HELTER SHELTER

A Lunatic Searching for Asylum

A memoir of sorts

Written with love by

Niki Smart

iMay Productions

Copyright © 2020 by Niki Smart

All rights reserved. No part of this book may be reproduced, scanned or distributed in any printed or electronic form without permission. Please, for the love of God, do not participate in or encourage piracy of copyrighted materials.
Purchase only authorized editions and you will make authors everywhere very happy—seriously.
Cover Design: Kelly Brown

To book the author please contact info@nikismart.com

First paper book edition June 2020

ISBN—10: 0-9856166-2-8

ISBN --13: 978-0-9856166-2-5

Publisher: iMay Productions

Helter Shelter

I wholeheartedly love being alive on this here planet mirth, however, I still carry a litany of grievances—things that piss me off. There's iceberg lettuce, diesel fumes, people who speak super loud on their cell phones, cyclists that hog the road (share the road applies to you, too), overpriced clothing, people that buy overpriced clothing, overpriced anything really. There's traffic, high-pitched wailing guitar solos (Lord no), stupidity, people with hacking coughs in airplanes or cinemas, poorly designed neighborhoods with maddening one-way systems, rudeness ...the list goes on, and on, but by far my biggest peeve are parents who mistreat their children. Man, that one just makes my blood bibble-bubble.

I'm sure you've heard the complaint that one has to have a license in order to drive a car, but to have a child there is no such prerequisite. Any asshole (or more accurately, any vagina) can birth a child. Wouldn't it be wonderful if parenting classes were part of the high school curriculum—a preparation for things to come? Simple parenting classes, with common sense things like: feed your child, wash your child, read your child a bedtime story. Children are truly a gift, and I'd like every parent to know this: your child starts off loving you more than anything in the world. You are the entire universe to your child. So much so, that if you lost one of your legs, your child would gladly lop off one of theirs to donate to you. I read that in a book somewhere, so it must be true. Honestly, their love for you is wholly unconditional, and your love for them should correspond.

These innocent, little humans look and learn, so make sure that when they're looking, you are modeling behavior you want them to learn. Lie to your child, and they will probably learn to lie to others (and in due course, they'll lie to you). Hit your child, and they will most probably learn to hit others (and eventually maybe even hit you). And here's something to think about: a child that's being abused by its parents, doesn't stop loving its parents. It stops loving itself.

I hold firm the belief that if everyone loved and nurtured their children appropriately, the crime rate would drop considerably. Imagine if my parents loved me and made me feel safe, secure, and valued. Would I really need to steal, lie, be violent, do drugs, cheat, rape? I honestly don't think so. If my parents truly loved and respected me, and through their unconditional commitment, I learned to accept and love myself—would I still grow up and have the need to shoot my spouse and my kids, and set the house on fire?

Okay, of course there are a few bad seeds out there—bad seeds that remain bad no matter how well we nurture, love and educate them. On the whole though, I'm betting the world would be a way nicer place if we could all be solid, loving, well-balanced parents. Work on that, okay? Yes, I will, too.

Please humans, let's love our children *and* one another—Amen.
Niki Smart
February 2020

This was written pre-pandemic, so I'm not sure that my "litany of grievances" are valid anymore. But still, they get the point across. Bad parenting leads to bad adulting, and that makes life shitty for everyone.

For Samantha ♥
Thank you for choosing me as your parent.
I love you more than words can express.

And
For all the children who passed through the shelter,
please know that you are awesome.
Yes, indeed.

MOST NAMES HAVE BEEN CHANGED TO PROTECT
IDENTITIES

Foreword 8

CHAPTER 1—The Blood Sucking Monster 12

CHAPTER 2—Dry Sausage Bait 20

CHAPTER 3—Shit Happens 28

CHAPTER 4—Painting a Brighter Future 34

CHAPTER 5—Staff Infection 39

CHAPTER 6—The Hoff 46

CHAPTER 7—Cut to the Bone 51

CHAPTER 8—Two's Company—Three's an Uncomfortable Reminder 55

CHAPTER 9—Delusions of Grandeur 61

CHAPTER 10—What happens in Vegas doesn't necessarily stay in Vegas 65

CHAPTER 11—Drugs, Psychopaths and Penis Issues 73

CHAPTER 12—Side Effects Included 79

CHAPTER 13—Love Song 83

CHAPTER 14—Vulnerable 88

CHAPTER 15—Don't Lift the Carpet 92

CHAPTER 16—Invisible 97

CHAPTER 17—Break up—Break down 101

CHAPTER 18—Round Two 110

CHAPTER 19—Captain, oh my Captain 115

CHAPTER 20—The Mourning 122

CHAPTER 21—Unfair Trade 130

CHAPTER 22—Sandbag Me 136

CHAPTER 23—Get a new Puppy	142
CHAPTER 24—Fight to the Death	152
CHAPTER 25—Slap some Veneer on it	161
CHAPTER 26—Missing	166
CHAPTER 27—Destitute	173
CHAPTER 28—What goes up must come down and vice versa	178
CHAPTER 29—Flip Switch	182
CHAPTER 30—Down and Out on the Town	187
CHAPTER 31—Lack	192
CHAPTER 32—Yo-yo, yoga	196
CHAPTER 33—Two Weeks of Bizarreness	203
CHAPTER 34—Revisiting the Blood Sucking Monster	210
CHAPTER 35—Peace out	216
USEFUL LINKS	220
ACKNOWLEDGEMENTS	222

Foreword

God dammit—where am I this time? I struggle to shake off the stupor I passed out in. Seems I'm in the passenger seat of my own car, and I'm alone. Okay, that's better than waking up with a stranger in my car, or waking up in a stranger's car, or waking up in a stranger's bed and not knowing where the hell my car is. Great—so far, so good.

My mouth's dry as gravel and a million blood capillaries throb out a torturous version of the can-can in my head, making it so I can't-can't focus. I raise an arm to adjust my glasses but they're not there. Shit! How come I always lose my glasses when I'm blotto? And why does my arm hurt? I examine my scrawny arm (resent the laxness of it) and frown at the bruises spreading on my upper limb. Dark ugly bruises, like someone grabbed me by the arm and meant business when they did. In reality, whomever it may have been was most likely only trying to help my drunken ass stay upright.

The passenger seat has been pushed back as far as it will go and I figure I've been comatose here for several hours. I assess myself further. My shirt's untucked, my bra strap's unfastened, and my jeans are unzipped—how thoroughly disagreeable. Essentially though, my clothes are on, and for that I'm grateful. I continue taking inventory, slowly, because each time I move my equilibrium needs a few seconds to catch up. My brain is mercilessly afloat in alcohol.

Scanning my car, I realize that my coat is also missing, although my handbag isn't. It's flung in the back seat with receipts from various bars spilling out. Double shit! I've undoubtedly drunk a small fortune away, and that's the last thing I can afford to do.

With a twist on the review mirror, I see my reflection and stare in shock at the matted, tangled mess that is my hair. To make it worse, there's an ugly bald patch on the right side of my head an inch above my ear. Looking down, now I notice the blonde hairs strewn everywhere. Sad, little disseminated strands of keratin proteins laid out bare and useless.

Okay, so let me get this straight. Someone grabbed me by the arm, threw me in my car, undid all my buttons, my zipper and my bra clasps, then stole my coat and glasses, and yanked my hair out?

This is quite possibly not exactly what happened, but to be honest (as per usual) I don't really want to know. I presume I'm most likely to blame, and the guilt, shame and self-loathing that follow my wild nights of debauchery are already bubbling forcefully within me.

I bring my seat upright to find myself staring at a brick wall. Whichever way I look, cold walls seem to glare disapprovingly at me. They also inform me that I'm in an underground parking lot.

Scooting into the driver's seat, I realign everything—my seat, my review mirror, my side mirrors. Someone's been driving my car. Someone's been fiddling with my clothing. Someone's been pulling my hair out.

Of all these things, it's the hair pulling that upsets me the most. I'm not down with people grabbing my hair because it comes out so easily. That makes it sound like people tug on my hair fairly often, which isn't true. What happens is it gets caught on a button, or a cufflink, maybe a bracelet, and with one swift avulse a bald patch appears. Having suffered alopecia areata as a kid, my hair tends to break off at the slightest provocation.

Tears prickle my eyes as I pick up each detached strand feeling immense regret. It's as if each ripped-out hair represents a wasted opportunity, a wrong turn, an irreparable damage. If I could cry my way back to a full head of hair, I'd have no problem here. If I could cry my way back to last night and have a do-over that would be swell. If I could cry my way back to healthier self-esteem, I'd sit in my car and drown in a sea of self-pity. Yes indeed, if I could cry my way back to a happier time, wouldn't that just be hunky-bloody-dory. But no, I just cry, and I'm miserable, and balding, and feel like the biggest loser.

Noting an exit, I turn out of the parking lot whereupon bright, white daylight hits me like a mini Hiroshima. God, I wish I had sunglasses. My eyes are melting. How am I supposed to figure out where I am with my eyeballs steaming? It doesn't help that I don't recognize the condos whose parking lot I've spent the night in, or that the names of the streets are not familiar to me.

I drive about aimlessly for a few blocks, until mercifully, Pacific Coast Highway surfaces and I realize where I am. I'm in Dana Point. Why? I have no idea. I head north, back to Corona Del Mar. Not exactly home, more a temporary base, but home for right now.

Being in the driver's seat, and thanks to the eye-scorching daylight, I now discern blood on the passenger seat. And I instantly know. Aw come on, seriously? Unfortunately, yes. I have bled through my feminine hygiene products, through my underwear, through my jeans, and I'm still bleeding right now, most likely sullying up my driver's seat as well. I literally convulse in self-pity and pull over to the side of the road.

It takes me several minutes to regroup, then I gather up the receipts from last night's festivities and spread them underneath my derriere. Quite right. Let me bleed all over my wrong doings.

All I want to do is shower and crawl into bed, although by the time I make it home, I no longer care about the showering part. Peeling off grubby clothes, I refresh at least my underwear and seek refuge under my comforter.

Lying in my singlewide bed, a desolate despair floods my very core. I hate myself. Really, really hate myself. I hate my life. I can't function anymore. I can't see a way to make things better. It's not that I want to kill myself; it's just that I no longer want to be alive.

That thought repeats itself over and over, as my chest collapses under a weight of hopelessness.

I whisper the words out to my empty room: "I no longer want to be alive."

Give me shelter from the storm
Keep me safe and keep me warm
Teach me how to be strong
So I can find out where I belong

The Shelter Song

CHAPTER 1

The Blood Sucking Monster

At 2:35 a.m. the phone rings. Shit-damn! When the shelter phone rings at this hour it can only mean one of two things: a) a heavy breather, or b) an emergency admittance. I don't mind the heavy breathers, I can hang up on those, but an emergency admit means I may actually have to *do* something; like extra paperwork. Yes, I'm horribly unmotivated and I may as well throw in bitter and pissed-off, too. Reason being: I pretty much hate my job.

Due to my complete lack of enthusiasm, I shoot my co-worker an imploring "can you please answer that" look, and bless his little cotton socks, he does.

"County Youth Shelter, Ben speaking," he says, smiling at me.

For his reward, I wedge a hand into my armpit and pump out some boisterous farting sounds.

Child Crisis Services is on the line and Ben speedily establishes that they've just evaluated a 13-year-old girl at a local medical center nearby. They've determined that she doesn't meet criteria to be admitted to hospital, but Child Services don't want to send her home either. Nope, because that's where all the drama-rama started. So they're hoping we can give her a bed at the shelter.

"What precipitated the hospital visit?" Ben asks.

I already know the answer to this: altercation with parent. 90% of the time this is the case. And, ding, ding, ding—we have a winner. Mom and daughter have had their first physical fight. Apparently, the daughter bit the mom on the arm, but the story's somewhat unclear because the evaluator's struggling to understand the mom's thick accent, and the minor's speech is groggy, as she's been sedated.

"I'll need to talk to both mother and daughter in order to get the minor into our shelter," Ben explains.

That is our policy at the shelter. Everyone who participates in our program has to first complete a Telephone Interview. It means we ask both parent and child a whole lot of questions, and they answer...or not.

The mother, Rowena, is first on the line. After gathering all the particulars: name, address, birthdate, dad's name, medication child is currently taking, Ben moves on to the tougher questions. "Can you tell me what happened at home this evening?" he asks delicately.

I can't hear the mom's reply, but I can hear that she's crying. This is standard. Once the parent opens up, the hurt gushes out. I watch Ben scribble down her responses in the column marked "Parent" on the interview form.

> Child attacked mother; mother stressed by work and overwhelmed; daughter doesn't listen. Nina's school performance dropping, stays out without permission, doesn't respect mother, Nina is uncontrollable...

Their situation mirrors a million others. The daughter has reached her teens and with that passage comes the testing of limits: the back talk, the disrespect, the disregard for rules and curfew. Naturally, Rowena isn't used to her daughter behaving this way. She wants her sweet, obedient, loving daughter back, but in order to grow up, Nina has to change. This is crunch time—the pivotal point where parents need to knuckle down and set clear limits, impose rules and regulations, and enforce boundaries. This is where parenting can become a true challenge, and sadly, many parents aren't up to the task.

I'm a fine one to talk. My own daughter, Samantha, who is 14 going on 25, (with the occasional regression back to 5) can trigger me effortlessly. I, myself, revert back to 5 at times, and that's when parenting becomes particularly problematic. How can I parent my child if I'm stamping my little feet and flapping my arms about in a huffy tantrum? In truth, at the right moment, a mere blink from my daughter can spark me to complete detonation.

KABOOM.

Ah shit, Samantha. Your mother just dispersed herself all over the living room.

Ben finishes up with Rowena and Nina comes on the line.

"Nina? You understand this is a voluntary placement, right?" Ben places his hand over the receiver to whisper, "she's drugged to the gills."

Lucky her. I'd like to be drugged to the gills.

Every child needs to give their consent in order to enter the shelter. They have to commit to staying for three weeks, and to working the program. Otherwise, what would be the point of them coming in?

"Nina, would you like to stay at our shelter for a few weeks? Nina? NINA are you awake?" Ben sounds pretty tired himself.

Through a muddled conversation, Ben manages to secure Nina's buy in, and sets her up to enter the shelter program. Rowena opts to transport her daughter herself although typically, emergency admits arrive by ambulance. Their ETA is in roughly an hour.

Ben continues with paperwork, while I reluctantly march upstairs to prepare a bed. Since Nina is coming directly from the hospital she probably won't have pajamas with her. I forage through our donation closet, searching for a clean pair of PJs. Nina is thirteen, but that doesn't necessarily mean that she'll be small. We've had thirteen-year-olds at the shelter the size of Ben and me put together. I grab a small, a medium and a large size to cover my bases.

The donation closet has unwittingly contributed a fair amount of clothing towards my own wardrobe at home. I scavenge through the donations when they arrive and anything that's unsuitable for the shelter and is roughly my size, or my daughter's, comes home with me. My comfy favorites materialized this way. Like my stripy jumper with holes in. You can't buy that at the GAP. Samantha is not quite as fond of her secondhand outfits.

I place fresh towels and a bedspread on the only empty bed left in the house. Nina will be rooming with 14-year-old Chelsea. Fearing that Chelsea might freak out in the middle of the night on seeing a body in the bed alongside her, I gently rouse her.

"Chelsea, there's a girl called Nina coming to sleep in here, okay?"

Chelsea nods a sleep-addled head. She probably won't remember me waking her in the morning. She's had her handy-dandy, sedating dose of Seroquel right before bedtime. Many of our residents are prescribed this anti-psychotic drug. It appears that psychiatrists are happy to hand out these brain-chemical altering drugs to children as if they were M&Ms. Okay, yes, there are kids who benefit from Seroquel, or similar drugs, but I'd wager that a healthy diet/life style and some proper parenting might do the trick, too. In my book (and this is my book), Seroquel is akin to a whack on the head with a sledgehammer...night, night kids.

I trot back downstairs to wait for Nina and Rowena to arrive. From the living room I have a view of the road, and since this is a small beach town, no cars drive by at 2 a.m. The streets are empty and quiet—that is until Rowena floors it past the shelter. I hear brakes screech a little way down the road.

"She's here," I call to Ben, who is holed up in the staff office doing that extra paperwork I'm niftily avoiding.

Realizing she's missed the shelter, Rowena swings her car around for attempt number two. She thunders towards the shelter...and me, as I stand waving my arms on the front porch to guide her in.

Rowena steers directly for the house. And I mean directly. She drives straight for me. I wonder if she plans to mow through the hedge and over the carefully planted garden right up to me. That would make for one hell of an emergency admit.

"Whoa!" I yell, holding my arms up. "STOP!"

The car shudders to a halt and everything goes silent. The front end of Rowena's car is now in our garden with her headlights beaming on me. The rest of the car juts out sideways in the street.

"Nice parking job" I mutter, as I plaster a happy smile on my face and approach the oddly parked vehicle.

Trancelike, Rowena clenches the steering wheel in death grip and I note the gauze wrap on her arm—ah yes, the bite. Next to her, the biter, Nina, slumbers peacefully in the passenger seat.

"Hi," I say. "Welcome to the County Youth Shelter."

Twelve years I've been at the shelter. Twelve years! Somebody bloody shoot me. No one has made it as long as I have, mainly because teenagers are exhausting, and, more to the point, the pay is super shit. My job of youth supervisor (as is my title) is a high turnover job because it's low-low pay, along with long-long hours and a fair amount of abuse hurtles your way on a daily basis. You're subjected to insults, foul moods, pretend farting sounds, real farting sounds, urine, feces, vomit, terrible body odors, constant whining and bickering, plus, eight hours of the favorite teenage saying "no fair".

On top of this, the position requires a degree because, as you know, a degree can come in handy when you're mopping up vomit. Hand in hand with the low-low pay is the low-low level of staff appreciation. For all our good work, we do not receive a Christmas bonus, or any bonus for that matter. Due to cut backs in the county, we've had no pay increase in years. What we do receive, however, is a patronizing letter from the headcheese every Christmas reminding us that the reward for our efforts are the warm fuzzies we get from helping others.

Hmmm—yes, but cash would be rather agreeable, too.

No one can handle the job for very long. I've seen the shiny, fresh-eyed employees arrive on their first day all set to make a difference. They go all out, giving it their heart and soul, and slowly, as they realize their job is an endless, thankless task, the resentment kicks in. Within three years, I myself began to think of the shelter as "the blood-sucking monster". A monster that takes, and takes, and takes, until you're utterly expended, and then it simply hires a replacement.

To save my sanity, I signed up for extra graveyard shifts. Firstly, you're paid an extra buck an hour, and secondly, the teens are asleep for the bulk of your shift, which makes it a hell of a lot easier (besides the pesky emergency admits). And thirdly, there's also only one other staff member to deal with, which keeps things simple. Nightshift sees me working from 11 p.m. until 7 a.m., after which I go home, sleep a little, and then have my day to do with as I please.

And what do I please? Well, to become a pop star of course. Makes sense, right? Reluctant youth supervisor by night and sleep-deprived wannabe pop star by day. All my training with anger management, oppositional defiant behavior, ADHD, drug issues, dialectical behavior therapy—that will come in mighty useful, don't you think?

I usher mother and daughter into the living room and hand Rowena the paperwork she needs to fill out. Her hands tremble as she takes the papers. I realize Rowena's whole body is shaking as she sinks onto the worn couch and surveys the room with fearful eyes.

"This is a nice place, yes?" she asks nervously.

"Fantastically nice, yes ma'am." *Unless you're a teenager who would rather chew glass then spend one night here.* "Why don't you fill out those papers while I show Nina her room?"

I give Nina her PJs—small. She is slight, with big brown eyes and pursed lips. She's pretty, except for the perpetual tight-mouthed look of disapproval. And disapprove she does—of everything and everyone. Nina's a hard sell on the shelter. She immediately insists that she never agreed to come in; that she was drugged at the time and hadn't realized what was going on, which is essentially true. Now she wants to go home.

I sympathetically remind her that things aren't exactly spiffy at home.

"How about you stay here for tonight, see what it's like? Maybe we can help sort out some of the trouble that's happening at home?"

"Why don't you keep my mother here then?" Nina snaps, her mouth pinching. "She's the one who needs help."

Nina could be right. The mom probably does need help. She appears to be scared of her own shadow. She even startles when we re-enter the living room.

"How do I get back home?" She asks me, her eyes wide with worry.

"Easy. From here you take the forest road and…"

"No. No forest road." She interrupts. "I need a freeway."

"The forest road leads you to the freeway," I explain. "It's the fastest way."

Rowena's worry intensifies. "No. Someone can carjack me on the forest road."

Right. This tiny village with zero crime rate is bustling with carjackers late at night.

"You're perfectly safe, I assure you." I try not to look contemptuous. It's easy to dismiss someone else's peculiarities as dippy but I have a fair amount of these bizarre, paranoid thoughts myself. I don't like driving over railroad tracks, or being in glass elevators. I'm afraid of cows, and midgets make me fiercely uncomfortable—so there you go.

"I promise you nothing will happen." I try to ease her worry. "There's never been a carjacking in this vicinity."

I doubt anything I say comforts her, but thankfully once she's completed the paperwork, Rowena climbs back into her curiously parked car and lurches off into the dark. Brave woman.

With Nina safely asleep in bed and her mother courageously navigating the forest road, I head back to the office where I plan to binge watch episodes of *LOST*, or *House*, or whatever I damn well fancy. This is why I switched to nightshift: way less stress…and work.

Ben suddenly giggles, which, if you knew Ben, you'd find quite adorable.

"What?" I ask him.

Ben swings his monitor to face me, hits play and a Japanese game show appears on the screen. There's a large wall with cutout shapes gliding towards contestants who balance on a plank above water. The contestants attempt to contort their bodies into the impossible cutout shapes heading their way, hoping to fit through and thereby avoid being knocked into the water beneath them. For some reason, this goofy Human Tetris game sets us off, and both Ben and I cry with laughter, punch drunk from lack of sleep. When a contestant sends the entire wall crashing over, we replay the segment time and again, laughing hysterically, until tears stream down our faces. I slap the desktop in a fit of glee, buckle forward in hysterics and am hit with the urge to pee because my bladder cannot handle this much hilarity.

As I stand up, a thump-thump sound comes from the staircase that I instantly recognize. I leap into the hallway just in time to catch Chelsea as she tumbles to the bottom of the staircase. Dazed and confused Chelsea throws her arms about my neck and clasps onto me.

"Mommy, mommy, mommy," she sobs heart wrenchingly.

"You're okay," I assure her. "It was only a dream. You're safe."

Chelsea whimpers against my chest as I quietly shepherd her back upstairs into bed. She's asleep again in a nano-second. I doubt she was ever fully awake. Sleepwalking (and talking) is fairly common amongst our clientele. Hell, some of these kids flop out of bed and spend the night face down on the floor. They sleep backwards, or with their heads dangling off the side of the bed. They wet the bed, they poop the bed, they attempt to sleep in each other's beds. I remember one child who came hurtling downstairs bringing her entire bedding with her. She had a full conversation with staff and at no point was awake.

Watching Chelsea and Nina's tranquil faces, listening to them breathe easy in sleep, I'm suddenly hit by a rush of those darned warm fuzzies. Hmm—the headcheese might have a point. My work here *is* worthwhile. I'm guarding these young children while they sleep and it makes me feel goddamn saintly.

So yes, I hate my job…and…I love my job.

CHAPTER 2

Dry Sausage Bait

Stepping into a coffin, that's what flying is like for me. Like being sealed into a goddam steel sarcophagus. I despise flying. Loathe it entirely—yes, far more than my shelter job. It's pure torture for me. Vacuum packed into a flying death machine that at any given moment could erupt into a fireball and incinerate me. Not my idea of a good time. This means that when faced with an upcoming trip to Tampa, Florida (fully paid for by air miles from a generous friend, and painstakingly organized by me), I chicken out at the last moment. I don't care that I've spent days planning this trip. I don't care if my friend has given me his miles. I care that I'm not going to be charred to a crispy delight. Illogical? I think not.

What is a lowly paid youth supervisor doing going to Tampa anyway? Remember the pop star part? Yes, well, I'd organized a few dates for myself to sing in various clubs in Tampa and I'd set up an interview on a local radio station. It had required complex scheduling to arrange all of this and then I go ahead and pull the plug on myself. What a lily-livered, chicken-shit I am.

My stress levels drop considerably once I make the decision not to go, but then my guilt kicks in. Still, I'm used to guilt. I know how to combat my guilt. I know exactly what to do. I call up my gal-pal, Shirley, and tell her we simply have to go out. In a flash, I'm at her door, knocking.

"Come in," she yells happily, because Shirley loves me. And I mean, she *really* loves me. Not lesbian-type love but weird I-frickin-love-you-so-much type love.

Shirley was a model when she was younger, a successful one at that. And no wonder, because she's gorgeous. She has impossible blue eyes and perfectly symmetrical features presented in a pleasing oval-shaped face. I'd probably go for the lesbian love with her if I were that way inclined. But I'm not, however, and honestly, I like Shirley simply because she's an adequately out of control drinker like myself. There's no fun in hanging with a teetotaler if you want to go get tanked. And tonight, I plan to blow up the tank.

Who bypasses the opportunity to do a radio show and play concerts in an all-paid-for trip? Apparently, I do. What would I tell the teens at the shelter if they were showing such a reluctance to follow through on their dreams? I certainly wouldn't tell them to go out and get their drink on. Nope. But luckily, Shirley isn't a youth supervisor, and she doesn't judge me.

I do, however, judge her. I judge her to be somewhat soft in the head because of her obsessive dog-crush. Sure, she loves me, but Shirley is besotted with her Australian Sheppard, Brody.

On my arrival, Brody leaps up, barks in excitement until my ears ring, and scratches the crap out of arms.

"Isn't he adorable?" Shirley gushes.

"Yes, I hate him," I say in an agreeable tone because I know this is touchy territory. Shirley loves that damn dog more than she loves me. Shirley loves her dog more than her husband. She does. She told me that if there were to be a fire, she would rescue Brody first, then her hubby. Hard cheese for the hubby.

Furthermore, Shirley is one of those annoying pet owners who imbue their animals with all kinds of human qualities. Consequently, Brody knows if she is depressed. Brody understands her needs. Brody is slightly psychic and can mind read. Apparently he even knows when his birthday is.

"He gets excited when I bring his cake in." Shirley says proudly.

Yeah right, what a bloody genius dog. No matter how much I explain to Shirley that Brody is merely picking up her excitement, plus the scent of something edible, she remains obstinately firm in the belief that Brody knows his birth date.

"So, if you forgot his special day, do you think he'd sulk, and avoid you, and think to himself what an uncaring cow you are for forgetting his birthday?" I ask, hoping this might help Shirley see how cockeyed her premise is.

She hands me a dog biscuit. "Here, give him this. Brody loves treats."

I have zero intention of giving Shirley's anthropomorphized beast from hell a treat and nimbly thwart her effort to form a bond between us by grabbing the biscuit and cramming it in my own mouth.

"Ha!" I smirk triumphantly at Brody, opening my mouth to allow him a view of the chewed-up mush in my mouth. That's right you shaggy shit: your treat—my mouth.

You can't blame me for disliking Brody. Not only has he scratched my legs and my arms, vomited on my feet, rammed his wet nose into my crotch area more times than is caninely decent, but he is also the reason that Shirley left my last birthday party early. "I have to go home. Brody is alone and missing me."

Come on. He's a goddam dog for Christ's sake. He can't tell time. He doesn't know how long you've been gone. He's not missing you. He's crapping in your backyard right now and striving to lick his own testicles. He's doing that unappetizing dog maneuver of dragging his butt across your lawn to scratch his irritated anus which is most likely itching due to worms.

What I should tell my friend is: "Look, I don't like having to compete with a dog for your attention. It's demeaning."

Instead, I say nothing, and imagine deftly zinging a blow dart straight into Brody's psychic neck.

Shirley finds it hysterical that I've eaten the dog biscuit. "Are you hungry?" she asks me. "Would you like another?"

The dog treat tastes like liver sawdust, and no, I don't want another.

In search of a snack for me, Shirley rummages through her kitchen cupboards and gleefully pulls out some South African dried sausage known as Droëwors. They are shriveled, dehydrated meat sticks that look fairly repulsive.

"Would you like some Droëwors?" she giggles.

We hardly knew each other back in Johannesburg, South Africa, where we both grew up. I'd heard of Shirley and seen her face in magazines, plus I'd worked with her younger brother (and when I say worked, I mean I sang with him at weddings and suchlike). Yet somehow, Shirley managed to stumble across me in Orange County. We planned a meet up and voila—firm friends. Hailing from the same country has a way of doing that. You "get" these people. You understand their lingo.

"Let's bring those with us," I suggest. "Imagine the men we can seduce with those babies." I pop open my eyeglass case and wrap two Droëwors in my cleaning cloth. "Why hello there, would you like to try my sausage?"

Shirley shrieks in delight and follows suit by shoving several Droëwors in her purse.

"Ready." She grins.

Our destination for the evening is a restaurant/bar in Corona Del Mar called "The Quiet Woman", and tonight, being Thursday, is "pick-up-a-slut" night. There's slim chance of meeting someone of high quality here, and I'm not really expecting to "land" me a man with my dry sausage bait. I am, however, fully expecting to mock several men and make myself feel superior to them by asking them to spell words like: diarrhea (which I know will be a miserable fail for most of them). I am also fully expecting to make them buy me drinks. The sausage line will break the ice, because seriously, who can resist Droëwors?

My flirting techniques may appear callous—making men spend money on me while I strive to humiliate them, but the bottom line is, there is a good chance I will have sex with them—so, there's that.

Shirley and I make our way to the bar area where sucky smooth jazz lilts through hidden speakers while loads of over-groomed Corona Del Martians check each other out. There's a rigorous effort being made here to appear sexy-cool. It's a style I can't quite manage to pull off myself. Fine, in that case:

"Hi. Can you spell diarrhea?"

"Uh...d...uh...i...a...is there an 'h'?"

I've met doctors who can't spell diarrhea. Makes you think doesn't it? No, not about unpredictable, explosive evacuating.

"The Quiet Woman" is packed so I beeline for a low table at the back where we can sit far from the madding crowd. This places us away from the action, but I'm okay with that. I don't care to mingle with these über-cool Martians anyway. I merely want to drink—a lot. Fortunately, I have the ability to consume vats of cheap wine without throwing up. My physique may not be overly impressive but my stomach lining certainly is.

I enjoy drinking. It's my go-to coping skill. It makes everything tolerable and takes the edge off after a long day of counseling teens at the shelter—teens that on occasion tell me that they hate me and that I suck big ass monkey balls. Of course, there is the remote chance that they may be right. Perhaps I do suck big time? After all, I have issues. Plenty of them. Issues up the ying-yang. Issues with body fluids, rules, textures, authority, farm animals, confined spaces, trust, and sadly, a rather Corona Del Mar issue with looks because when a short man approaches my table, my inner bitch starts clacking: "I'll bet this guy has short man syndrome—the Napoleon complex; the aggressive *I have to prove myself because I feel inadequate* stigma. And that's quite the receding hairline. How are his eyes so closely set together? Keep walking buddy, you're so not my type."

The short, balding, closely set eyed man smiles sweetly. "My friend and I are leaving and wondered if you wanted our seats over there?"

"Sure. Thank you." I say, and open my eyeglass case just for the hell of it. "Would you care to try some sausage?"

He gives a slight start as he squints at the Droëwors. "As incredibly tempting as that looks, I'm going to have to decline the offer." He smiles again, and I note the little crinkly lines next to his eyes that give his smile an extra twinkle.

"You are a wise man," I praise him.

Shirley and I join him and his friend at their table, and they don't leave. Instead they order more drinks and I happily drink myself tranquil. I listen as my new short admirer sparkles out stories. He's entertaining and funny, and I find myself drawn to him. He appears to be drawn to me, too, because when his friend leaves, he stays put.

Come the end of the evening, Shirley takes off, and I drag my newfound interest to my car where I force him to listen to my latest CD. I'm keen to make a lifelong fan out of him, and once he's heard my incredible talent, surely the man will be hooked for life? Yes?

My musical abilities must have some impact because after listening he suggests we stroll down to the beach. On the other hand, I may also simply have an aura that reads: "easy lay—she's desperate!"

The air temperature is at its summer best. The ocean shimmers picture-perfect under the moonlight. We frolic about in the sand, and finally hoist ourselves up into a lifeguard tower. Who knows? I may soon be tempted to make out with this man even though he's short, balding and lacks the golden ratio for facial beauty (supposedly, faces are most attractive when the features of one's face reflect phi in their proportions—yes, like Shirley's face).

We're doing some flirty chit-chat, when he starts talking about his latest film project. My ears prick up. Wait. Back up. What was that? A film project?

He tells me that although he recently sold a screenplay to Disney, he's worried because so much can go wrong before the screenplay will ever see the light of day.

"I've already been paid," he says, "but I want the film to get green lit." He stares out over the glistening water.

Paid? Holy-hand-grenade. The man has sold a screenplay...to Disney. I try to stay calm and play it sexy-cool like the Martians.

"I was meant to be in Florida tonight playing on the radio," I blurt out. It's like I can't help myself. For some reason now I really *need* to impress this man and my music career is my only ammunition. Besides, it is sort of true. I should have been doing a radio interview tonight, except I wouldn't have been paid for my time, and the radio station was a mere piddling outfit, certainly not Disney.

Shit. My music career is not impressive at all. I hurriedly shift the attention back on him.

"Act out a scene from your movie." I say, trying to concentrate through my alcoholic fog. I suddenly wish I hadn't had that last glass of wine. Unexpectedly, the man my inner bitch thought I wouldn't be attracted to, is worthy of focused consideration.

He starts telling me the plot, the sub-plot, prattling away and wig-wagging his arms about for emphasis. He's charmingly engaging, but I struggle to keep my eyes open. It's approximately 2 a.m. and my brain, awash in alcohol, is basically turning to slop. I lean back against my raconteur and his arms wrap around me. It feels good. I'm happy to pass out on the beach and spend the night under the glorious moonlight with him. Maybe he senses this.

"I think it's home time," he says. "I have to get up early."

Damn it—foiled again.

Back at my car he hands me his business card, and in return I scrawl my number on one of my CDs and give it to him. Let him have a musical reminder of my wonderfulness.

Strapping me safely into my car, he asks, "Are you okay to drive?"

"Sure am," I lie.

He leans in and pecks me on the cheek—a tame goodnight kiss.

"Well, good night then, Niki Smart," he says.

I wake to a throbbing hangover. Nothing new there. I wonder how I made it home and a nauseous glance out the window of my mobile home verifies my car parked askew in the driveway (not quite Rowena style, but still...). Relief flushes through me, which is rapidly followed by a severe self-rebuking. I'm a goddam menace to society. Shame on me for driving in that state. Shame on me for drinking so much. Shame on me for being bloody irresponsible. Was I trying to get a DUI? What about my young daughter? How could I be so reckless? And what about my shelter job? If I got a DUI I'd probably be fired. Like my guilt, this self-loathing is familiar territory.

Sitting up in bed, I notice a piece of Droëwors on my floor. Had I enjoyed a midnight snack? Or had I simply flung withered meat sticks about my bedroom for shits and giggles? On picking up the sad-looking sausage, a crumpled business card falls to the floor. I must have passed-out with it clasped in my hand. I straighten it out to read the name:

Roy Hoffman.

The beach conversation comes flooding back and I leap from my bed with greatly improved vigor. I'm eager to Google this man. I'm eager to Google him good and proper.

CHAPTER 3

Shit Happens

By the time my shift starts, my hangover has subsided—thank you, oh slightly engorged, hardworking liver. I read the logbook to find that Nina's been informing staff (in colorful language) that she's ready to go home. On being told that this probably won't immediately happen, Nina opted to let loose a few more choice expletives, then withdrew to sulk and pout. Not surprising behavior from one of our teens. They are damn near experts in the swearing, sulking and pouting department, although Nina does pack an extra impressive rudeness. Within a short period of time she has managed to piss off the entire staff and all her peers to boot. The minute I leave the safety of the staff office, she attacks me, too.

"Those jeans make your legs look fat," she informs me as I enter the recreational room.

Clever girl has hit my weak spot. I'm super self-conscious of my legs, believing them to be riddled with cellulite and unfit for public exposure. On top of that, I haven't fully recuperated from my late night and am a tad fragile. Still, I don't react.

"How are you doing today, Nina?" I ask cheerfully, making a mental note to retire my pants from my jean pool.

Nina doesn't bother to respond. She crosses her arms defensively and slumps deep into the couch.

"I understand it's difficult for you to be here," I attempt to engage her. "If I were your age, I'd probably hate it here, too."

This only stirs her up. "Why can't I go home then?" she scowls.

"It's not that you can't go home, you can, and you will. But when you do, we want to make sure that things go well. So while you're here, we want to help you understand how your behavior affects the way your day pans out."

Nina stares angrily at the floor.

"Maybe we can't change our circumstances, but we can choose to change our reaction to those circumstances." I'm speaking to dead air. Nina is not listening.

"Like your thighs are fat and you can't change that, but you could change your jeans?" She sneers at me.

Ah, so she is listening.

"Not exactly," I smile brightly, while part of me itches to slap her smartass face. "More like now I get to choose my reaction to you saying my thighs are fat. I could cry about it, or I could shout at you. I could laugh…see what I mean? I can't stop you insulting me, but I can choose how I react to your insults."

I feel victorious. I've handled this well.

"It's not an insult." Nina stares defiantly at me. "It's a truthful observation."

Like I said, working with teenagers is exhausting. They are relentless.

Another new resident, has entered the shelter, Malcolm, a chubby, rather large for his age, 12-year-old. Malcolm seems happy enough, smiles a lot, and interacts well with the other kids. Nina has already meted out the "you are too lame to even contemplate" eye-roll at Malcolm, but it doesn't seem to perturb him. In fact, Malcolm smiles constantly and seems impervious to any ill will against him. He has a round, happy face, and it's hard not to like him. Except, when I go over to talk with him, I notice a smell. A smell I recognize. Quite simply, Malcolm smells of poop. Not like poop, but *of* poop. I have a good nose, and since I actually poop on occasion myself (no, say it isn't so) I can clearly identify the offending aroma.

"Hey Malcolm. Do you want to play basketball in the backyard?" I ask him.

He nods his big smile—yes.

Other staff members join in and once Malcolm is fully absorbed in playing basketball, I sneak up to his room to investigate. Sure enough, the noisome whiff is even stronger in there. In the corner, I notice a small trashcan stuffed full of toilet paper that's already served its purpose of wiping botty clean. I presume that Malcolm has pooped in his trashcan, but on further wary investigating, I see that there isn't any poop in it, merely the poop-soiled toilet paper.

"What's his game?" I wonder. "Where did he put his poop?"

I head back downstairs to write about my discovery in the logbook and recommend that the therapist on duty call Malcolm in for a chat. Meanwhile, I dig out his file and start reading about how Malcolm was severely abused at age two. I don't get very far because I hear Nina causing trouble in the front room. Duty calls, so off I go.

I'm working a double shift so I'm grateful when 10 p.m. hits and the kids settle in for the night. I'm tired and cranky and hope that nothing happens during the night. No emergency admits, no crisis situations, no meltdowns…just calm please. The only hitch I can foresee is a resident called George. He's a sweet kid, no problem at all, but he has a bladder issue. Lots of our residents wet the bed at night, and since they're teenagers (meaning they are painfully self-conscious), they're horribly embarrassed when they do. We discreetly help them change their bedding and assure them it's no big deal. But this kid, George, is a serial bed-wetter. George is a little different from the other bed-wetters in that he wets his bed every night due to a bladder deformity, not because of emotional stress. And although this young man has been seen by ample urologists, no one has found a proper solution for him. The solutions thus far have been that he sleeps on rubber sheets, wears a diaper to bed, and doesn't drink liquids after 9 p.m. In order to help George, the graveyard shift has been instructed to wake him up at 2 a.m. and force him to visit the bathroom.

That will be my job tonight. I will have to wake George to prompt him to void his bladder. The small hiccup in this is that George takes a large dose of that "handy-dandy" Seroquel at 9 p.m. that knocks him into next week.

At 2 a.m., I stand alongside George's bed and shake him lightly. His therapist has stressed that we approach him gently so as not to frighten him because George has been beaten by an alcoholic father, and usually late at night. Although the father is currently in prison (and has been for a while), George still has nightmares about him.

"George. It's time to use the bathroom," I say softly and shake his rather substantial body. George is overweight, as are a lot of kids that come through our doors. Thanks fast food restaurants and crappy school menus.

The gentle approach has very little effect. Shaking him lightly does exactly nothing. I shake him harder—still nothing. I prod and coax, tug and shove, and realize that I can sit George upright, shout at him, shake him vigorously, and he still won't wake up. He'll merely slump over again, fast asleep.

I try singing him a song. A sort of reverse psychology: a lullaby to wake him up—nada. I tell him there's a party going on in the living room—niet. He is not faking sleep. He is out. I give up and in the morning, George's bed is wet and pungent. As we change the sheets together, I assure him that wetting the bed is common and loads of kids at the shelter have the same problem.

"I'll try wake you again on my next shift." I say.

He gives a faint smile. "Thanks."

I'm glad that Nina doesn't know about George wetting his bed. I'm pretty sure she'd nail him to a cross. We can keep it hidden from the other residents, but the poor guy wets the bed no matter what we do.

George stretches to tuck in the last corner of a clean sheet and his T-shirt rises allowing me a glimpse of a red inflamed ring around his lower abdomen.

"What's going on with this rash here?" I ask him. "It looks painful."

George self-consciously adjusts his T-shirt.

"It's my piss…irritating my skin. The doctor said to put Vaseline on it, but that doesn't really help."

Poor George. The acidity of his urine is burning into his tender underbelly.

I want to help George. I really do. I step into the therapist's office.

"Hey Gwen. I just want to tell you that it's almost impossible to wake George. I try. I shake him, I shout in his ear. It's like he's in a frickin coma. The poor guy sleeps in urine almost every night."

Checking through George's file, Gwen points a well-manicured finger at his medication chart.

"Hmm, yeah, Seroquel. That'll do it." She contemplates. "Why don't you set off the fire alarm in order to wake him?"

Fire alarm? Really? And freak all the kids out? I have to stop myself from blurting out sarcastically "Why didn't I think of that? Oh, you therapists with your crafty methods." Instead I say, "That might upset the other residents? No?"

"I'm joking," she semi-smiles.

But I'm pretty sure she isn't.

Sure the therapists mess up, they're human, but on the whole they do good work. For example, take Gwen's diagnosis for the smiley-faced, foul-smelling Malcolm. I've finished reading his file and am now aware of the severe sexual abuse he suffered at the young age of two. Gwen's impression of Malcolm is that with no help in sight, he was unable to develop beyond his emotional maturity level of two. And what do two-year olds like to do? Sometimes they like to play with their own poop. Not wanting anyone near him, Malcolm started filling his pockets with feces, a sure way to keep people at bay—I can vouch for its effectiveness.

Clever Malcolm. This is his most excellent ploy in staving off unwanted attention. For years, Malcolm has been pocketing poop in an attempt to keep a protective distance between him and any possible perpetrators. Next time you tell someone they smell like shit, stop for a moment to consider why. Perhaps they too are merely trying to save themselves from being further molested or abused.

Just so you know, pooping and emotions go hand in hand. Think about it. When you're nervous, anxious or scared, or if you're in emotional turmoil, your guts tend to instantly liquefy. Say you walk in on your partner cheating on you? You may feel the urge to evacuate your bowels right there and then (and I, for one, advocate that you do so). You may even need to do a vom-poo—a simultaneous expulsion of vomit and diarrhea. Yes indeed, our emotions can send our bodies into total meltdown status.

There are some people who lose governance over the matter of evacuating altogether. We've had such a case at the shelter—Tracey, a 15-year-old who had no control over her bowels, resulting in her regularly pooping in her pants. Known as Encopresis, this is not an uncommon ailment, but Tracey had an added inexplicable symptom. She was completely unaware that she was evacuating her bowels. Even at the beach, dressed in a swimsuit, she let one go and walked back to the shelter unabashedly unaware that her suit was swinging low, loaded with excrement. Staff swiftly wrapped her in a towel and hurried her back to the shelter for a shower and masses more therapy.

It's true—your emotions and your bowels work in sync. Maybe when you are that desperate *not* to feel your emotions, you're willing to lose the ability to feel your bodily urges as well? What do you think happens to kids when they are abused, molested, neglected, ridiculed and carelessly unloved? Think they can handle it and simply "get over it"? Think again.

I sympathize deeply with these teenagers. These young folks have to deal not only with appalling home lives but also with the out-of-whack medical issues that result from their uneducated handling.

Be that as it may, somewhere in the back of my mind I fantasize about placing crap in my own pockets for my next outing to "The Quiet Woman" in Corona Del Mar. My fantasy is fed by the restaurant's sexist emblem of a busty woman without a head—that's why she's quiet. Does it represent what men in this area are looking for—big boobs, no brain—show me your tits and preferably shut up?

Well, with shit in my pockets, I'll speak in my own quiet, odiferous way.

CHAPTER 4

Painting a Brighter Future

"**I** want to paint my room maroon," Samantha informs me.

"Sure thing, Manthy" I smile at my daughter. "As long as you mean *you* want to paint, and not, you want *me* to paint your room."

"Brooke said she'd help. We can do it in one day."

I'm not too keen on this idea. It sounds messy and I'm pretty convinced that my 14-year-old daughter and her friend, Brooke, will tire halfway through the process and give up. Naturally, it will be left for me to finish. That's how most things end; with me left holding the baby…literally. I've been a single mother from the get-go, holding the baby with a mixture of resentment, adoration, terror and pure love.

My impregnator did, to his credit, offer to marry me but I chose not to go that route. I'd no interest in getting married. I was young and still brimming with pop star plans. Husband? No thanks. Baby? Sure, I'll give that a whirl. Fourteen years later, the husband part sounds a lot more appealing because holding my very lovely baby, as lovely as she has turned out to be, is often overwhelming for me. My paltry salary from the shelter hardly covers my rent, and strapped for money and stressed about how to make ends meet, it's hard for me to relax and simply enjoy my child. Quite the opposite, I often find myself yelling at Samantha because her few demands seem too gigantic to surmount.

"Mommy, can Elsie spend the night?" Samantha asks harmlessly. And my mind erupts into a statistical panic that goes something like this: Elsie is large and therefore she'll eat a lot of dinner and breakfast (that I'll have to supply, Jesus Christ). And she'll probably want to shower (which will use up hot water and shampoo, God dammit), and for sure she'll take a fresh towel (that I'll then have to wash, shit). I'll probably have to drive her home (which will chew up my gas, double shit) and, and, and....

"No, I don't think so!" I snap at poor Samantha, imagining that Elsie's sleepover is about to destroy my bank account, wreck my last strand of sanity and basically ruin my life. This crazy thinking of mine sees Samantha spending time at her friends' houses instead of them coming to us. I much prefer this arrangement and ship Samantha out whenever possible. This way the other family bears the expense and I gain a free babysitter. How horrible am I?

Adding to my "turn-me-into-the-worst-parent" stress, is the fact that Samantha and I are in the USA illegally. I brought Samantha here from South Africa when she was 3 because our country was having a bit of a blood bath. We came to America on visitor's visas, but those visas lapsed 11 years ago, and recently, a lawyer informed me that I should marry an American before Samantha turns sixteen. Once she is sixteen, it'll prove much more difficult to incorporate her. There'll be extra paperwork (and you know I loathe paperwork), plus, it will be much more expensive (yeah, don't even get me started).

I need to find a husband pronto, but this is no easy task. I struggle just to find a date. I don't quite fit in here, in Newport Beach, where we live. I'm not conservative. I'm not rich. I'm not busty. I'm not interested in painting my nails, or my face. It's hard to snap up a marriage partner when I'm a fish out of water. But dang-it, the pressure is on. I must marry, I must earn more, I must become a pop star, I must be a good mother, and I must, I must, develop my bust, or no guy will ever notice me (at least not in Newport Beach).

Brooke is the only kid I don't mind having over to spend the night. In fact, I love it when Brooke comes over. Brookie (as I call her) is 3 years older than Samantha and they've been firm friends since they were 6 and 9 respectively. They do the sweetest things together, like cooking, baking, knitting and art projects. They even took a sewing class together and made quilts with their names stitched on. It warmed my heart.

Before I bought our mobile home (for the enormous sum of $18k) Samantha and I lived across the street from Brookie and her people—the Moore family. In the afternoons, young Brookie would sit outside her house on the pavement, scuffing at the dirt, looking melancholic and bored.

"Go ask that little girl to play with you," I suggested to Samantha.

"I'm too shy," Samantha said (which was/is true).

"I think she'll be happy that you came to say hello. And you might make a new friend."

After some deliberation Samantha finally trotted over the road with me spying on her through the kitchen window. I watched Samantha's little blonde head bobble about as she chatted enthusiastically, and soon, Brookie's face lit up, and BAM—a life-long friendship was formed.

Brooke's parents spend long hours at work, meaning Brooke is often alone. Samantha and I are happy to take her in, and strangely, I never go into my habitual statistical meltdown over Brooke. She is simply a pleasure to have over. Plus, I feel sorry for her because her mom and dad are too busy to take her to the beach, or to the snow, or to go roller-blading, or even swimming—I invite Brookie to join us in almost everything we do. We call ourselves the three musketeers. To this day I feel like Brookie is my second child. She, in turn, introduces me as her "fairy godmother" to her friends, and yes, I'm rather proud of that title.

I agree to the maroon color and buy the necessary supplies, counting out every penny. A little extra money remains from my small budget, and on a whim, I buy some paint for myself, too. While the youngsters listen to the Spice Girls and transform Samantha's room to a dark plum color, I brush my bathroom into red and white stripes. It takes forever and my arms ache by the end of it. There's no way the girls will finish their job. This is truly hard work.

I peek into Samantha's room and there they are, happy as maroon-room-painting girls can be. A couple of splotches stain the floor, but they've done a seriously snappy job. They even thought to put down newspaper (which is more than I did), and there's only one small spill on the actual carpet.

Well done, girls. I salute their tenacity and their obviously well functioning serotonin levels.

"It looks great," I grin from the doorway giving them two thumbs up. I throw in a toe for good measure. "Two thumbs and one toe up," I commend them further. "How about we go swimming? It's stinking hot in here."

It is hot and I can see Samantha and Brooke are both glistening nicely. Our mobile home has the capability of reaching hellish temperatures, and swimming in the ocean is free, so what the hey?

They turn me down. Not unusual.

"Fine, sweat away. I'll go by myself." I reproach them.

But I don't go by myself because going to the beach alone isn't much fun. I feel self-conscious in a bikini and imagine that everyone is staring at my flabby thighs thinking "oh no, no, no…cover those up". For some unknown reason, I feel secure if Samantha and Brooke are with me, and my thighs bewilderingly firm to normal.

Fine, I'll stay home and hang with my girls even if they don't really want to hang with me.

I'm lonely. I don't have any "real" friends in Newport Beach. On top of that, Samantha and I have zero family members. We only have each other—our extended family is scattered all over the globe. This is mega-shitty, because I don't have anyone that I feel comfortable enough with to ask for help. I have no back up plan and no back up savings. I don't have anyone that I actually want to be with other than Samantha and Brookie. Even Shirley is only good as a drinking companion. Is it any wonder that I long to meet someone? I'm desperate for a support system. I'm waiting for my knight in shining armor. I'm waiting for my prince to come. He will come…won't he? I've waded through a boatload of frogs and zilch so far. Which reminds me that my latest potential, Roy Hoffman, has not called. That doesn't mean he won't...does it?

I don't recognize that I'm pinning all my hopes and dreams on an entity that I have no control over. That I'm "giving away my power" so to speak. That I'm willing, and wanting, to make another person responsible for my joy and my wellbeing. That I'm hoping for a quick fix by Mister Magical. I don't acknowledge that this is a big, fat cop-out, and that it's highly unlikely that I'll ever meet someone who can miraculously transform my less-than-perfect life circumstances into the life that I believe I should be living. The life where I wake with a smile on my face every day. The life where I'm happy, rich, content, successful and surrounded by loving family and friends. The life where I don't need to stress about rent every month. The life where both Samantha and I are legal citizens and able to travel in and out of the country (that way we could visit some of our actual family members). The life where every day is filled with blue skies, rainbows, and whopping-sized lollipops.

It simply doesn't enter my consciousness that no one can supply everything I desire, or more importantly, that no one should be asked to do so. Nor does it enter my consciousness that if I want someone fantastic, I better make sure that I am fantastic myself. What guy would want to date a dirt-poor, undocumented, single mother, who lives in a mobile home and believes she can yet be a pop star at age thirty-eight? Hell, I wouldn't want to date me. I'd avoid me like a plague of feathery warts.

There's a long, long journey ahead of me, and meanwhile I'm stuck in my lonely, desperate, sweat lodge, ignorantly aiming to marry a miracle worker.

I pop my head back into Samantha's room, "Hey, you guys should come and check out my bathroom. Oh, and I made some sandwiches for all of us."

If cheese and bread can bring me the companionship I desire, so be it.

CHAPTER 5

Staph Infection

Every Tuesday afternoon there's a two-hour staff meeting at the shelter that I affectionately call "Staph Infection". In a way, these meetings are infectious. I love going to them…and…they make me sick. When I first started at the shelter, I felt honored to sit amongst a group of caring individuals who strove to help the damaged youths of Orange County. Back then, I wanted to work at the shelter more than anything—well, no, not more than being a pop star—but still, I was so gung-ho to work at the shelter that even knowing that I was illegal and that there would be a required FBI check run on my background, it still didn't deter me. Imagine my terror when an FBI investigator called to say he needed to talk with me.

"It's not as dire as you think," he added.

He was right. It wasn't that dire because my legal status was never mentioned. Instead, he asked about a time when I'd been arrested for biting my then boyfriend. Had I known that biting my ex would be considered an assault with a deadly weapon and would see me in a holding cell with a $10,000.00 bail to pay, I probably wouldn't have bitten that young man. Perhaps I should warn Nina about the consequences of biting? Perhaps I should warn Roy about my deadly teeth? Perhaps I should work on my anger issues?

After guaranteeing the nice FBI agent that I wouldn't be biting anyone ever again in my life, least of all the kids at the shelter, he kindly gave me a "clean slate" and permission to work at the shelter.

To this day I've remained true to my word and have not bitten another soul. Seems my urge to bite has vanished completely, but sadly, my burning desire to work at the shelter is vanishing, too. Now I sit in staff meetings silently machine-gunning criticism at my co-workers (except Ben—I could never say, or even think, anything bad about Ben. That would be like bad-mouthing a bona fide angel).

I've listened to the same "problems" week after week. I've watched the same staff members suck up to the therapists at each meeting. I've heard our director scold us for every little thing and every big thing, yet I haven't noticed much improvement. For example, the director will say, "Don't write excess information in the logbook. We all have to read the logbook so just log what's important and make sure to sign your name to it."

Sounds simple enough, yes? Well, there is always (and I mean always) some staff member who enjoys writing essays in the logbook; volumes of useless information. Possibly they think that the rest of the staff simply can't do their jobs adequately without a lengthy explanation of what, where, whom, and why, neatly laid out in flowery handwriting.

A short log would read: *Client X returned from outing with parents. All went well. Pockets checked.*

A long log would read: *Client X was brought back to the shelter by her mother and father at 4pm. Client X told staff she had a good time, was chatty and seemed happy. Client said they ate burgers for lunch and asked if she could change her clothes due to spilling some ketchup on her top. Staff gave her permission to change after they had checked her pockets for contraband.*

Is what she ate for lunch or spilling ketchup vital information? Probably not.

During my years at the shelter, I've heard the request for short logs a million times. The problem is that the request is never directed at any one specific person. If our director simply said "Sally, cut down your entries in the logbook", that would make it easier. We could all give Sally a filthy look and move on. But it's not the director's style to single anyone out. Our director, Colleen, started out as the shelter secretary, but because she's a hard worker and genuinely put her heart and soul into the job, within a few years she became the head of the shelter. I've nothing but admiration for Colleen, and I understand that she throws out these "blanket complaints" so that no one in particular is being scolded or made to feel uncomfortable. The annoyance in this though is that the person who the complaint is truly aimed at usually doesn't realize that the director is talking about them. I watch their face as Colleen delivers the admonishment because *I* clearly know it's them. *They* are the guilty party. By their facial expression though, I can tell that they're agreeing with the director, and probably thinking, "yes, some people do, do that". The guilty ones simply don't compute that it is them the director is talking about.

"Don't sit there nodding, idiot," I itch to yell at them. "She's talking about you."

When I first started at the shelter I assumed that every catch-net complaint was aimed at me. Luckily, I grew out of that phase fairly quickly, and now rest comfortable in the knowledge that I am perfect and that everyone else must be doing shit wrong. Do you think perhaps there is someone sitting opposite me thinking "Quit your nodding, fool. It's you she means."

The teens attend the first segment of staff meeting, and today, as is typical, they have sat as far away from staff as possible. The girls squash together on a couch, the boys on another. They have to sit separately; it's one of the shelter rules. Boys and girls cannot sit next to each other, but Ben and I can, and we do. We sit alongside each other because Ben also hails from South Africa, and us South Africans, we like to stick together.

Let me just tell you that Ben has über blonde hair, striking blue eyes, and the patience of a Zen Master. He might well be an actual angel, and though I'm way older than Ben, I seek his sage advice all the time. So yeah, I sit close to Ben, and if you could, you would, too. The rest of staff (about another fifteen people) are scattered around the living room on the mismatched furniture.

Every staff meeting begins with our newest residents reading us their "This is Me" paper. This is a brief questionnaire that each teen fills out upon entering the shelter, then they read it aloud at their first staff meeting. The questionnaire finds out the following information about our clients:

1 – Their name, age, and who they live with.
2 – The reason why they entered the shelter.
3 – What they are most proud of about themselves.
4 – What they hope to have accomplished once they leave the shelter.

Nina is first up with her "This is Me" introduction paper.

"I'm Nina. I'm 14 years old. I live with my mother and younger brother. I came to the shelter because I got into a fight with my mother and I bit her on the arm."

Yes, she did. She bit her mother, and being bitten by your daughter is not funny, yet I find I have to stop myself from smiling. Come on, it's a little bit funny, isn't it? How funny would it be if Samantha bit me? Oh right. Not funny at all. How funny was it for my ex when I bit his chest? Again, not that funny.

"I'm most proud of myself for being nothing like my mother." There's venom in Nina's voice. "And when I leave the shelter I hope to go live with my dad." She flops back down onto the worn couch as staff applaud her efforts.

Next, it's George's turn to present. He reads his paper in a bold voice, basking in all the attention.

"My name is George and I am 16 years old. I live with my mother, my brother, four dogs, two cats, my mother's boyfriend, a hamster and God."

The "This is Me" papers are fairly revealing. I take note of the order of relevance for George. The mother's boyfriend is listed after the dogs and cats and is only a notch above the hamster. And religion must play a large part in George's home life as God is mentioned as a family member.

"The reason I came to the shelter is because I keep arguing with my mother's boyfriend. He's a douchebag."

Colleen promptly sets him straight. "Let's find a nicer way to express that. Like, you don't get along with him."

George squints at her. "Yeah, I don't like him at all. He's an a-hole. Can I say that?"

"Just letting people know you don't like him is enough." Colleen smiles kindly at George. "What are you most proud of?"

"I'm most proud of myself for my karate," George says. "And when I leave here, I hope to have a better attitude towards my family."

George eyes Nina, hoping he has impressed her, but she merely rolls her eyes, demonstrating that she considers him completely lame, along with everyone else.

I love that George is most proud of himself for doing karate because he's a hefty lad and physical activity is obviously sorely needed. Which makes me wonder if there will ever be a law saying you can't overfeed your children. I believe it's a form of child abuse—allowing your children to stuff their faces. I once saw a young boy at a restaurant eat six tubs of ketchup along with his French fries, and his mom didn't bat an eye. The kid was huge and lumbering. That's no way to spend a childhood; wheezing and sweating, too fat to do anything.

And yes, I'm being judgmental. But make no mistake; I realize how very far from perfect I am. How would I fair if I had to fill in the "This is Me" questionnaire?

1 – I'm Niki. I'm 38. I live with my 14-year-old daughter in a rather disgusting mobile home park.

2 – I entered the shelter in hopes of easing the suffering of vulnerable children because I used to be one of those children. In reality though, I probably haven't worked on my own shit enough to be of dependable use.

3 – I'm most proud of my musical abilities, but if I'm honest (which I'm not) my relentless desire to be a "famous singer" is slowly sucking the joy out of my life.

4 – When I leave the shelter I hope to be married to a wealthy, handsome, sexy, smart, completely understanding man who cherishes me above everything—plus, I want to enjoy a huge recording deal that results in a staggering musical career.

Reasonable expectations, right?

The last resident to read his "Me I see", is Malcolm. He has clean pants on (staff have checked his pockets for feces) and judging by his happy face, you'd never suspect he'd been through so much.

"I'm Malcolm, I'm 12 years old. I live with my uncle, five cousins and my grandma, who owns the house. I came to the shelter because my uncle thinks I'm touching my little cousins."

He keeps smiling brightly, which is pretty disturbing, and has staff shifting uncomfortably in their seats. I, for one, wouldn't be at all surprised if Malcolm *was* touching all over his little cousins. After all, someone did exactly that to him.

Once done with their introductory readings, our young residents are sent out of the room while we continue with our staff meeting. We start on client management, first hearing the background of each teen, then discussing their treatment plan. We plot the progress of our current clients by sharing our observations of them and we make recommendations for them. How are they interacting with the others? What does staff notice about client X while working on the floor? How can we best serve them? What are their strengths? What are their weaknesses? We voice our concerns and make suggestions for each client. It's a team effort—it takes a village.

We hear that Nina's mom (Rowena) hails from a Middle Eastern culture where women don't count for much. Where women are beaten by cruel (and feasibly, sexually repressed) husbands. Where women must cook and clean, and are basically second-class citizens. Rowena was married by the age of 12 and had two daughters by the time she hit 15. This abusive husband beat her frequently until the day he attacked her so brutally that she landed up in hospital. A family member helped Rowena and her children flee the country, but naturally, Rowena was traumatized. Even though several years have passed, Rowena is still terrified that her husband will find her. Living in constant dread and overwhelming fear has left her mistrusting the world. Rowena finds it hard to fend for herself, never mind fending for her offspring. She behaves like a child herself: a scared little girl.

Unfortunately, a scared little girl can't take very good care of another scared little girl, and Rowena's helplessness has forced Nina to become the adult. This damaging role reversal leaves Nina brimming with resentment. She doesn't want to forgo her childhood in order to take care of her mother's unmet needs. As payback, Nina punishes her mother by voicing how she longs to go and live with her father.

We finish up case management with our last client, George, and I suggest that we try to concoct some type of catheter for him. What about a sort of condom that snaps over his Johnson and opens into a balloon? The other staff members snicker at me, but I'm being wholly serious.

"Why can't a doctor design George some kind of apparatus?" I ask, aiming my question at no one in particular. "The guy's sixteen. How's he ever going to have a girlfriend? Or a bed that doesn't reek of urine? How is he supposed to get a good night's sleep? How can he lie down for a few hours without having acid burn into his lower abdomen and buttocks?"

I sense everyone looking at me, but can't stop myself. "The only answer his mother has come up with is to make him sleep on newspapers on the floor. She claims to have spent hundreds of dollars on mattresses, so really, she's only solving her spending problem because sleeping on newspapers isn't a proper solution for a young man, is it?" My face is getting hot and red. "That's more like a solution for a badly trained pet."

The room goes silent at my flare up. Staff meeting is not the appropriate venue for venting. I imagine the other staff are thinking: "Really? We're going to snap balloons and condoms over this boy's shaft? Yeah, child services would love that."

CHAPTER 6

The Hoff

How long must I wait for this Roy Hoffman fellow to call? Can I call him? What is the proper protocol for someone raring for a mate? Frantic for a savior? Having fully Googled my potential lifesaver, I've learned that the deal he signed with Disney was in the six figures. To me, that's six figures of no more shelter job necessary, rent paid for the rest of time, life altering, party-til-the-cows-come-home capacity. The Internet won't give me more information, but unless those six figures are 000,000, I think my new friend has earned quite a nice sum of money. Strangely, his short stature and odd features are remarkably diminished by his bank account. Apparently I can date a short, balding, squinty-eyed man after all. Who knew?

Um, so what's the difference between me and the Corona Del Mar/Newport Beach gold-digging women that I detest? Yes, exactly.

Although he has my number, Roy has not called, and because I'm exceedingly impatient (and disturbingly desperate), I decide to call the number on his card. Doubt kicks in as I pick up the phone. I'm nervous. What if he doesn't remember who I am? What if he is with someone else? What if, what if, what if? I punch in the numbers, and due to the gut-linked-to-the-emotions thing I was telling you about, I'm hit with the urge to poop. Dammit.

"Hello?"

"Hey Roy." Quell those bowels. "This is Niki. I met you at the..."

"Niki Smart!" he shouts, joyfully interrupting me. "I was going to phone you today."

Bugger me. I should have waited. Still, he sounds pleased to hear from me. I'll take that as a good sign and get straight to business, because, how long can I postpone my intestinal demands?

"I'm playing a gig at the Gypsy Den on Thursday night. Would you like to come boo me?" I try to sound casual as I throw this out, then hold my breath.

"Sure. I love your CD. I'm listening to it right now. I'm busy driving to San Diego."

My heart does a happy little jig. He's listening to my CD right now. In some mysterious time/space dimension he is with me at this very moment. Oh fabulous day.

We solidify our plan to meet and I hang up elated. I'm pleased as pie that Roy has agreed to come to the Gypsy Den, and for some unknown reason, I feel like I've won some form of a victory. Yes, like I'm a real winner because Roy's coming to hear me sing. Furthermore, I'm childishly flattered, and ever-so-pleased, that he's listening to my CD.

Inexplicably, I have the urge to buy something for Roy. This is a sure sign that I'm liking this man, because with my budget, I never want to buy anything for anyone. I am not a giver. I'm more of a taker. Perhaps it is my nature, perhaps it is my situation—it remains to be seen. Be that as it may, off I trot to the one place where I can afford to shop. The dollar store.

And glory be, at my dependable dollar store, I find the most splendidly fitting gift for Roy. For 99 cents I buy him a business card holder that's in the shape of a typewriter. It's perfect. I can't wait to give it to him, and to see him again, and to have him watch me perform, and to have him fall in love with me, and to have him marry me, and to finally get my life going with galloping gusto. Yes-ah!

Thursday night arrives and I set up my gear at the Gypsy Den, a laid-back bohemian venue in Santa Ana. Even though I've been singing and playing guitar for years, I still get nervous every time I play. Tonight is no exception. As usual, it's all about me. Will the audience like me? Will they want me to shut up? Will they be able to appreciate the sheer talent billowing their way? Probably not—bunch of tone-deaf imbeciles.

I'm so wrapped up in my disdain for mankind's obvious lack of musical appreciation that I completely forget about Roy coming to my gig. I play my first set to polite clapping (I'm not bringing down the house here), and I'm on a break when Roy appears. The minute he sees me, he throws his arms in the air and calls out with enthusiasm "Niki Smart!"

Maybe it is the sound of my own name said with such eagerness. Maybe it's the twinkle in his eyes. Maybe it's the cute way in which he greets me. Maybe it's the pitch of his voice or the giant smile he serves up. I'll never know for sure, but suddenly something deep inside me bursts into sunshine and leaves me beaming stupidly at Roy.

"Hi...uh...you," is all I manage.

My performance anxiety skyrockets as I play my final set for the night, primarily because I need Roy to think I am amazing. I really, really need him to. Why? I don't know. I just do. I feel like a schoolgirl when I look at him. A foolish, giddy, teenage girl (signifying that perhaps I should be a resident at the shelter, not a supervisor?) Suddenly, I feel young and vibrant, and anything seems possible. Well, as long as he likes me back. That thought pleases me immensely—Roy liking me back.

I play my strongest songs; the ones I know elicit the most applause. I do my utmost to appear confident, at ease, and incredibly pop star-ish. Come on, fall for me, rich Disney-dealing dude. Fall for me.

I finish my set, thank the lukewarm audience and quickly pack up my gear, trying to look sexy as I wind up my cables and unplug my speakers. Then Roy says some magical words:

"Would you like to grab a drink across the street?"

Would I? Would I? I absolutely bloody would, because I want to spend more time with Roy Hoffman—and, I *love* drinking.

Roy does all the right things. He opens the door for me, sits me comfortably at a table in the outside patio area, orders me a drink, and asks my permission to smoke a cigarette. I tell him it's only okay if I can smoke one, too.

I light up and puff away while sipping on a chilled glass of chardonnay. Soon the combination of cigarette and wine sends its welcome calm through my body. I need that calm. This Roy-boy is unnerving me. His mere presence is pushing me to be as witty, interesting and supremely stimulating as possible. I see a chance to "strike" when some German guys come up and ask if they can sit at the table next to us. I pick up their accent (which is no big effort for me since my mother is German) and I seize the opportunity to answer them in perfect Deutsch.

"Kein problem, nehmen sie platz, bitte."

This evokes a quick German conversation with the usual: how do you know German *(Woher kenne Sie Deutsch)* question, and the: my mother was born in Garmish *(Meine mutter wahr in Garmisch geborn)* answer. I know Roy is watching me and I'm absurdly pleased to have a chance to show off my linguistic skills. In truth, my German is rather shabby.

"I didn't know you could speak German" Roy says, obviously somewhat impressed. "You are quite a surprise."

"Ah, Roy Hoffman. There are a lot more surprises in store for you." I smile coyly at him. Atta girl.

This seems like a good moment to surprise him further, to prove my point.

"For example, this" I say, and whip out the typewriter/cardholder that I've wrapped in colorful paper and topped with a bright red ribbon.

"What's this?" he asks.

"I bought you a present."

The smile on his face is worth every single penny I spent. That's right—all 99 of them.

"I should have got you something," he says.

Darn tooting mister.

He rips open the present and marvels at his new business card holder. "Where on earth did you find this?" He laughs.

This is not the time to be honest. I can't let him know how cheap I am. Unable to come up with something quick enough, I use a tactic oft employed by the teens at the shelter. I eye my neighboring table's food, and I distract.

"Did you know that eggplant is called Aubergine in England? And pickles are known as gherkins in South Africa?"

His face lights up on this information, like I've just handed him a key to the universe of knowledge. What I've really handed him is a manipulative magician's maneuver to divert his attention from what's really going on. If he asks about his present again, I'll use the humor ploy and tell him I shoplifted it from Pier One.

"I love your accent." He smiles his crinkly-eyed smile at me.

No matter how withered a heart has grown, I imagine that encountering Roy's smile would have to make an impact on it. His smile sure works on me. Before I can edit myself, I blurt out, "You smile with your whole face. It makes my solar plexus happy."

This evokes a loud belly laugh from Roy, a laugh that is every bit as pleasing as his smile. It simply bubbles with joy. My solar plexus is in heaven.

Shit. Oh Shit. Help me...I'm melting.

By the end of the evening, all I want to do is set up another time to see Roy Hoffman. My own heart unwithers as it swells with renewed hope. It's physically painless, but emotionally, it floods me with a mix of unbelievable optimism and gut liquefying trepidation.

CHAPTER 7

Cut to the Bone

Our latest client is thirteen-year-old Lucy. She lives with her aunt and uncle and came to the shelter because she cuts. Given that this is a "crisis intervention shelter" we deal with teenagers intent on self-harm on a regular basis. Our shelter is classified as a high-level of care facility, meaning that we have to ensure a fully safe-proofed house. There's no glass in our picture frames, our cutlery is locked up, the lampshades are made of canvas materials (not glass), and we don't use paper clips. You'd be appalled at the depth of damage an innocuous paper clip can cause. As for pens, pencils, and scissors, well, they can only be used under strict supervision for obvious reason.

"Recently my cutting's become more intense." Lucy tells us during her "This is Me" reading. She rolls up a sleeve to show us a bandaged arm. "This time, I needed stitches *and* staples...I cut through to the bone."

Is that pride in her voice? Does she want admiration? Sympathy? Help? Is she looking to shock us? It's hard to tell. What I do know is that if we have one cutter at the shelter, there's a good chance that it will spark another teen to follow suit. Cutting seems almost transmittable between teenagers, and I already see the fascination with which the other residents are eyeing Lucy.

Why is cutting so popular? I understand that when kids are inundated with intense, overwhelming feelings, slicing into their skin can bring instant relief. Teens cut for various reasons. It can be a way to stymie emotional pain, or it can be a form of self-punishment with an "I-deserve-this" mindset. I'm worthless, I'm ugly, I deserve to feel pain.

Cutting can be a way to feel in control, or a way to feel more alive. People cut for a myriad of reasons and the intensity with which they cut differs, too. Some cuts are superficial, while others can be life-threatening gashes, like Lucy's.

We make Lucy sign a safety-contract while at the shelter. This contract promises that she will let staff know whenever she has the urge to cut, so that we can hopefully intervene and help her deal with her anxiety in a healthier way.

When we discuss Lucy's case it comes to light that Lucy's mom was recently arrested and incarcerated. That's why Lucy is currently living with her aunt and uncle, but she feels unwanted by them. The main reason, however, that Lucy's cutting has ramped up is because her aunt and uncle live in a different district meaning Lucy can no longer hang out with her friends, or her boyfriend. Lucy lost her entire support system overnight.

Staff is told to help Lucy identify her strengths. Does she like music? Dancing? Cooking? Sports? Reading? We're told to help her find positive ways to self-soothe. Fortunately, Lucy likes to cook and soon she's helping prepare tacos with Ben in the kitchen. It's rather lovely to observe this hard-edged child soften as she relaxes into chopping up cilantro and deep-frying taco shells. The shelter residents sit down for dinner—it smells delicious, the place is cheerful, and we share a meal of tacos and laughter. I'm struck by how simple it is to please people. A tasty meal and attentive company—that's not a big ask, until I think of mealtimes with Samantha. I cook, nothing smells good, Samantha berates my cooking skills, and then we eat in sullen silence. Thinking about this, I realize my home life is deteriorating into a gloomy mess and I instantly check my phone. Has Roy left me a message? Does he want to take me on another date? Hello Roy?

I get the teens settled for the night and because I'm overly worried about George, I make a concerted effort to wake him at 2 a.m. After about 10 minutes of shaking and pleading, I manage to rouse him.

"George, time to go use the bathroom."

He blinks up at me and I know. I'm too late. George is already soaked in urine. Resisting the urge to quip, "You're in urine" I usher him to the shower, turn the faucets on, set the temperature, and step aside.

"I'll be right out here, ok?"

He nods at me.

Five minutes later, I knock on the door. Nothing. I wait a little while and knock again. Still nothing.

"George?"

No answer. I try the door, but George has locked himself in.

"George? I need you to open up." I bang on the door. Nada, nichts, niet.

Heart pounding, I race upstairs to the office and grab the universal key. Thankfully, we have special locks on the doors precisely in case this sort of thing happens. I clatter back downstairs and fumble at the lock, hands trembling, until finally, the door pops open.

There's George, fast asleep, slumped over in the bathtub. His body is blocking the drain making the water rise around him. I reach in and vigorously shake him awake. It takes George a moment to wake and fully comprehend where he is. He stares at me in horror then quickly clamps a hand over his privates. Poor kid is mortified. Naturally, I don't care that he is naked. I care that he could have drowned in the fricken shower.

I report this incident in the logbook, and early the following day, when the director reads my entry, George is discharged. The director deems him too high risk, saying staff can't keep him safe; that we can't help him. And she is right. We really can't help him, but I feel quite strongly that we should try to find someone who can. Okay, maybe urology is not our area of expertise, and granted, we are not allowed to touch our kid's parts, but I don't like giving up on the boy.

If he were my son, I would design him a goddamn catheter. I'd find a way. I would.

Yes, I get fired up on behalf of our clients. My heart goes out to these children who suffer through all kinds of horridness.

CHAPTER 8

Two's Company—Three's an Uncomfortable Reminder

Roy does invite me on another date, and another, and another, and soon my whole day is preoccupied with obsessing, pondering, imagining and fixating on Roy. When I'm with him, I'm filled with insuppressible energy and immense good humor. I'm so fucking positive I could rupture from the sheer wonderfulness of it all. My heart starts singing the minute I set eyes on him. I float, I glide, I fly, I soar. I fall deeper and deeper, head over heels, stone cold in LOVE with Roy Hoffman.

I have never felt such intense love for anyone. It's all-consuming. It's a real high...and I mean real as in an actual physical biological and biochemical high. My brain's awash in neurochemicals (yes, yes, and sometimes alcohol), and the ventral tegmental area in my brain is churning out dopamine. My prefrontal cortex is flooding with norepinephrine. My hypothalamus is secreting Oxytocin and Vasopressin. Ladies and gentlemen, I am on a "lover's high."

This new love sucks up my entire focus, leaving little room for Samantha. Obviously I love my daughter, but it's a different kind of love—a maternal, protective, unconditional love. I don't fixate on seeing her the whole day or wonder if she'll like what I'm wearing. Quite the opposite. Samantha is about to turn 15 and not at her most pleasant. Since our relationship has been down sliding for about a year, I'm not that keen on spending time with her at all. And I can almost guarantee you that Samantha will detest whatever it is I'm wearing.

To top it off, she has implemented a new DON'T policy.

"Don't speak to me, don't touch me, don't look at me, and don't breathe on me" have become her new rules for any of my attempts to engage her. These new rules leave limited room for bonding, and although I can sense us drifting apart, I'm not sure how to "save" us.

I do completely understand though. Samantha is at the stage where she needs to individuate from me. She's preparing for a future where I won't be by her side to "fix" everything for her. She needs to break away from me in order to survive. It's a normal process, one I see enacted daily at the shelter—parents horrified that their little Johnny is suddenly telling them to "fuck right off". The teens at the shelter sometimes tell staff the same sort of thing, but I don't mind other peoples' children telling me to "die, mother fucker, die." Let me assure you that it's vastly different when your own child unleashes lavish amounts of hatred at you. It's ow, ow, ow.

Samantha and I no longer hold conversations. I ask questions and she merely grunts gruffly at me in a semblance of what may be an answer, or may be a request for me to drop dead. It's hard to tell.

Listen you little brat, who the hell made you? I did. Who the hell has fed you and clothed you all these years? I have. Who the hell has played chauffeur, nurse, chambermaid and ATM machine for you? Me, I have. Who has compromised their entire life for you….uh …okay, actually not me, I haven't. More accurately, I've forced Samantha to live the way I want, which means, we live on a shoestring budget because I refuse to take an extra job in case it hinders my chances of becoming a pop star, or impedes my creativity. In my mind, budding pop stars need flexible hours—it makes sense to me, okay?

When Samantha tells me that she doesn't like Roy, I don't pay attention. I don't listen, because, come on now, Samantha doesn't like anything I like anymore. Not the way I dress, not the food I cook, nor the words I use. It upsets her if I say the word "gangbanger." Why? I have no idea. Not that I use that word very often. Or "alky" (slang for alcoholic). She hates that one, too. No, I don't use that word very often either.

Samantha thinks I'm dumber than a blunt rock and that I have the dress sense of a garbage disposal. She has further kindly illuminated for me that I smell like "an old woman." Now, bear in mind that I'm 38, dress like a goddamn rock star, and that my brain (in my not-so-humble opinion) is a finely tuned device...when I'm sober.

Possibly, Samantha is right about the smelly thing though. I am a bit lax in the laundry arena. I wear my clothes until they practically come to life. As I mentioned earlier, doing laundry costs money, and that fact quickly puts the kibosh on clean clothes every week.

Since Samantha finds me vaguely repulsive, her dislike of my new boyfriend is not surprising, plus, I like him enough for the both of us.

This dynamic translates to Roy, Samantha and I not spending time together as a unit. It's either Samantha and me, or Roy and me. There isn't much overlap and I don't push for it. I don't enjoy spending too much time with Samantha anyway since her full-blown teenage modus apparendi is to hate me no matter what. Obviously, it's much nicer for me to spend time with Roy who tells me I'm charming, that I look like a pop star, he doesn't think of me as "a smelly old woman", and evidently loves being with me.

Those are our completely in-love faces (although Roy's is a little trickier to decipher)

On top of this, he spoils me with dinners, flowers, movies, drinks and even pays to have my car washed. He fills my lonely life with a magic that anchors me firmly on cloud 9. Actually, I think it's more like cloud 9999—I have never felt so completely content.

I pity everyone else around me because they don't have what I have. They don't have a partner that brings euphoria to even the most mundane. They don't have a Roy Hoffman…I do.

"He's a jerk" Samantha snips, when I invite her to join Roy and me for dinner. "Besides I have a date with Bobby. He's picking me up in 10 minutes."

Bobby is a tubby, brash, un-evolved, egghead who has a postnasal drip and I loathe him. It makes me sick to think of him pawing at my daughter. Perhaps this is how Samantha feels when she thinks of Roy and me together?

"Where are you guys going?" I ask cautiously, knowing full well this is thin ice I'm treading on. Samantha could lob "sneer" grenades my way at any moment.

"We're going to hang out at Taco Bell," she says coldly.

I dislike the thought of my daughter loitering at Taco Bell as much as I dislike the thought of Bobby pawing her.

Samantha reads my face. "Why don't you like Bobby? There's nothing wrong with him."

"You guys always go to Taco Bell."

"So?"

"It seems so uninspired."

"What do you know? All the kids hang out there—it's a lot of fun. Last time we all spat in a cup, placed bets, then Danny drank it for $5."

My body gives an involuntary shudder. This information is a massive affront to my body-fluid issues.

"Drinking each other's spit is not what I'd consider inspirational. It's insanely disgusting." I shudder again. "If you want to go to Taco Bell, then I'll need you and Bobby to do an art project before you leave." I pull out some blank paper while Samantha scowls resentfully at me.

"How about you guys draw an underwater scene, then you're free to go."

Samantha grabs the paper out of my hands.

"God, you're so annoying!" she hisses at me. "This is ridiculously retarded, I hope you realize."

I don't realize. I think I'm pure genius. Force that Blobby to be imaginative, to use his brain, to match up to my daughter's creative capacity, while simultaneously setting limits and displaying an example of inventive parenting. Brilliant.

"I love you." I smile at her. "Please be home by 9 p.m." And with that, I head out the door for Roy's apartment. It's all very well that I set limits for my daughter; I just don't set any for myself. I would live in Roy's pocket if he'd let me. I'd marry him tomorrow. I'd drink a cup of his spit if he asked me…hang on, no I wouldn't—and that fools me into believing that I do have boundaries.

Dinner with Roy is wonderful, but I barely eat. I'm too excited to eat. I'm not hungry for food, I'm hungry for Roy—and no, I don't mean in a lewd sexual way. I mean it in a: I've been starved for this kind of companionship/attention/stimulation for many years" kind of way. He regales me with amusing stories and I devour every word. I drink in every nuance of his lovely, lively face. I soak in his animated body language, consumed by his hands sweeping, curling, and slapping. I want to absorb his very being. I'm deeply besotted. Please God, allow me to have this man telling me stories (even if they are the same ones) for the rest of my life.

I laugh with Roy, drink with Roy, smoke with Roy, and love on him immensely. I feel no guilt that I've left my daughter home alone with Bobby with no more rules than "draw a picture." Yeah, brilliant parenting.

Returning home, I find a beautiful drawing of a subaquatic scene propped up on the dining table. Colorful fish swim through gleaming seaweed, delightful sea horses hover in the background, and near the ocean floor a scuba diver and a stingray have a face off. I'm touched, and my regard for Bobby bumps up a tiny notch although in my head

I'm thinking: "Samantha drew this. Blobby probably just did some coloring in."

I once saw Bobby leap onto the hood of his car, jump up and down, and dent the hood well beyond repair. This "dented" an instant low opinion of him into my mind. Spoiled Newport Beach kid, given car by parents and trashes it—young, dumb and violent. Not my cup of tea. In truth, the car was about to be scrapped and Bobby was just having fun. He is not spoiled, or dumb, or violent. I am, however, old and judgmental. Let it be known that I do feel bad for consistently underestimating Bobby's capabilities and his worth. Let it further be known that Bobby proved me wrong and blossomed into a lovely young man.

Well done, Blobby.

CHAPTER 9

Delusions of Grandeur

Being in love makes working at the shelter so much easier. It makes everything easier. I'm viewing the world through radiant, gold-tinted lenses, and lo and behold, the world is now a shining, glorious place. Let the kids whine at me for eight hours straight, I will easily endure it. Let the kids act up, cry, provoke each other, swear, break rules—no problem, little friends. Let the kids empty their bowels into their waste paper baskets—I welcome their feces. Let Samantha cast her looks of pure disdain in my direction, I will smile and...nope. It still hurts. No matter how sunny my love-engorged disposition has become, her contempt for me still stings.

The newest shelter resident, Veronica, a gangly 15-year-old, ambushes me the moment I walk in the front door.

"I hear you play the guitar." She stares at me without blinking.

"Why yes I do." I beam at her, overflowing with love and thinking how sweet it is that she wants me to play her a song, or perhaps teach her a few chords.

"Well, I'm going on tour with Justin Timberlake," she practically snarls at me. "I'm his backing vocalist." Her stare intensifies.

Okay. I did not see that one coming.

"Great," I say. "Good for you, how exciting." I quickly brush past her and make my way to the staff office.

"What's the deal with the new girl?" I ask Ben.

"Veronica? She has delusions of grandeur."

"Her stare is a little disconcerting." I add.

Ben nods in agreement.

As far as delusions go, thinking you're about to embark on a tour with Justin Timberlake is not as crazy as thinking you're God, or believing yourself to be the Queen of England, still, I'm curious to hear this girl sing. I feel I can give her a fair evaluation since music is my arena, and who knows, perhaps Veronica is an awesome performer? On a subconscious level though, I'm somewhat miffed because, let's face it; *I'd* like to go on tour with Justin Timberlake. I grab the shelter guitar (a beat-up nylon string with loose pegs that can no longer hold the tuning) and go in search of Veronica. She's in a corner, humming to herself.

"Let's sing a song together," I suggest. "Name some songs you like to sing."

After a quick discussion, we settle on a Sheryl Crow song: "Are you strong enough to be my man?" *Well, are you Roy, dammit?*

Veronica can sing, but not fantastically. Not well enough to be going on tour with a major star. Not well enough to be going on tour with anyone. Backing singers are typically incredible singers, or super hot, usually both. Veronica is neither. I kind of figured, but I simply had to test her. Nonetheless, I don't question or probe her any further. I know that when these poor kids choose an altered reality it's because their own reality is not something they can handle. I'm not about to poke holes in her safe haven idea of touring the world with a gorgeous, famous man. If I want to collapse this reality of hers, I'd better have an even brighter one waiting to replace it, or Veronica might snap. And I, for one, certainly don't want to be the cause of "snapping" someone.

I learned this lesson early on at the shelter from 14-year-old Brendon when he refused to take his meds. Brendon was so adamant about not taking his meds that I reckoned there must be some deeper reason for his refusal other than defiance. I wanted to know what it was, so I pushed. Not because I wanted to help him, but because I wanted to satisfy my own curiosity.

"Why don't you want to take your meds?" I asked.

"I just don't," he sulked.

"You realize that these meds will help you feel better, right?" It sounded logical enough to me.

"Whatever." Not to him, I guess.

"Well, that's why they've been prescribed to you." I persisted.

Brandon crossed his arms taking a defensive stance. "I don't want to talk about it."

I should have left it at that. He was making it clear he didn't want to discuss this, but noooo, I ploughed on. "Your mother pays a lot of money for this medication, this stuff isn't cheap."

"I don't care." He said, clenching and unclenching his hands. "That's her problem,"

Ignoring his agitation, I pressed on. "She's only trying to help you."

And bingo, I sparked the trigger-button because Brendon swung towards me, his face contorted in a caged animal look of frustrated fury.

"Do you want to know why I don't want to take my meds?" he screamed at me.

Well, yes, clearly I really did, but the sheer intensity of his mood silenced me.

"I'll tell you why," he continued screaming as he wrenched his T-shirt up to reveal two swollen, dark-purple nipples. "Those meds make my nipples discharge and they fucking hurt." Brendon jerked his T-shirt back down, his eyes brimming with angry tears. "And I don't like having titties."

Brendon was taking Chlorpromazine—side effects: can make your nipples hard and discharge. Not fun at all if you're a 14-year-old boy. I could hear him sob as he ran down the hallway.

My regret was immediate and intense. I shouldn't have kept harping on like that. I'd forced him. I'd pushed him. I'd invaded him. Oh my God, I'd behaved like my mother. And for me that's a bad, bad thing.

Lesson absorbed, hence, I don't "push" on Veronica. Having satisfied my curiosity about her singing capabilities I feel no need to question her any further about her tour with Justin Timberlake. Instead, I spend my shift daydreaming about Roy while listening to Veronica sing every NSYNC song ever created. Eight hours later, my musings shift from Roy giving me squeezes to me squeezing Veronica's neck to help her shut up. 'Tis true, I'm not very magnanimous near the end of an eight-hour shift.

Other staff members assess Veronica. They ask her questions about record production and record contracts, and Veronica can answer them all. She has done her research. Then a most curious thing happens. Veronica's mother comes in for a family session and corroborates the story.

What?

For the briefest moment I'm flooded with jealousy. Sorry lady, but there is no way your awkward, off-key daughter is singing anywhere other than her shower stall. If I can't make it, how the hell can she?

Yes, my ego is pathetic.

Following several family sessions it comes to light that mother and daughter have a shared psychosis, an infrequent and extraordinary diagnosis. Shared psychotic disorder, also called "Folie à Deux" (folly of two), is a syndrome in which delusional beliefs are transferred from one individual (the "inducer" or "the primary case") who already has a psychotic disorder, to another with whom they have a close relationship. The closeness plays a large part in shared psychotic disorder and usually this closeness exists in relative social isolation. With no one to bump up against their delusion, it had continued to expand into their actuality.

My childish jealousy immediately turns to pity for this sadly misguided and lonely mother/daughter team. I don't stop to notice the similarity in their clutching at fame to save them from a glum life, to my own "pop star dream", or my rapidly growing fantasy of me being married to a famous screenwriter, attending red carpet events and taking Hollywood by storm.

Delusions of grandeur...cough...I have no idea what you're talking about. I have to go home and call Roy. Maybe he wants to take me to dinner tonight.

CHAPTER 10

What happens in Vegas doesn't necessarily stay in Vegas

Fortuitously, Roy does want to take me for dinner, and during the meal, I tell him about an observation day that I have coming up working with autistic youngsters. These kids, ranging in ages from 5 to 7, all have fairly severe autism. I'll be spending the day with them in a classroom located in Fullerton.

"Fullerton?" Roy says. "Why that's halfway to Las Vegas."

Well no, it isn't really, but who am I to disagree?

"I'll scoop you up in Fullerton," he grins "and we'll drive straight on to Vegas."

Good people, here is an offer I cannot, will not, would not in my wildest dreams refuse. I can't stop smiling—seriously. Roy's Las Vegas proposal has transformed me into a rare and mysterious "Grinning Monkey Orchid" (sure, go ahead, look it up).

With our Vegas plans in place, I bounce into the Special Ed. classroom full of vigor. There are fifteen students in all, and because I'm in such high spirits, I simply want to embrace the lot of them. As the time passes, however, my jubilant desire to connect turns into a concerted effort to avoid all closeness. One little guy has a runny nose and he's pretty much slathered in mucus by the end of the first hour. He wipes his nose on his hands, his sleeves, his shirt, his pants and the desk. I steer clear of him as best as I can. Another student spends most of the day with his hands shoved firmly down his pants, constantly scratching. He gets a wide berth, too.

There is limited cooperation from the class but not because the children are defiant. Quite the opposite. These kids seem to respect their teacher and want to please her it's just that they find it difficult to stay focused and on task.

I'm introduced to the class and can tell I'm about as interesting to them as a pot of boiling leeks. Moving freely (and cautiously) about the classroom, I observe the kids as they draw and attempt to write. This is a different world to my shelter. A whole other ball game, though equally as exhausting.

"Robert, take your hands out of your pants."
"Jeremy, come and get a Kleenex."
"Shelly, stop eating the eraser."
"Robert! Take your hands out of your pants."
"Jeremy, for God's sake. Wipe your nose."
"Shelly! Spit that out."
And so on, and so on.

After lunch, the children have an outing to the school library. They are encouraged to pick out a book and then get comfy on floor pillows to read their chosen title.

Sara, a cute Japanese girl, chooses a fairly advanced copy of Cinderella and reads it aloud to me, word perfect. She reads the entire story beautifully and I'm impressed.

"Cinderella's sisters aren't very nice, are they?" I say, attempting to engage Sara.

But Sara stares blankly at me and begins to re-read the book aloud to no one in particular. Sara's teacher informs me that although she is only 6, Sara can read at the level of a 10-year-old—however, Sara can't understand the meaning of what she's reading. I find it fascinating that Sara's brain can recognize and pronounce the words perfectly but can't knit them together as a whole to form a picture.

Back in the classroom the kids have their final period, music class. Everyone sits on the floor and sings "The Rainbow Song", complete with various actions of the rain pouring down and the sun streaming out. The kids sing with enthusiasm, staging a fine performance, and it's adorable. I'm quite moved by these little human beings who struggle so hard to do what comes naturally to most.

The school bell rings, and class is over. I thank the teacher, and remembering that Roy is waiting for me, I flat-out sprint to the front of the school. And there he is. My heart expands at the sight of him.

Sitting happily in the passenger seat, I tell Roy all about my day. I love that he listens, I love that he's interested. I just love. Oh love, love, love.

Fullerton is not that close to Las Vegas (as you probably know) and after a few hours of driving, I nod off. The kids have worn me out.

Suddenly, Roy slams on the brakes and yells "Oh Jesus! Watch out!"

I bolt upright, my heart pounding in my ears.

"What?" I stare ahead confused. There is nothing in front of us except a clear road. Roy starts to giggle, then laughs harder and harder until he's whooping in delight.

"I got you. Boy, I got you good!" He grins from ear to ear.

I, on the other hand, can't even muster a smile. This is not funny.

"You should see your face," he brays. "Priceless."

I say nothing. What is there to say? That his behavior is juvenile and imbecilic and that he almost gave me a fucking heart attack? That this must be a guy thing? That no girlfriend of mine would pull a stunt like that and think it is amusing. Or would they? Maybe I *am* sour grapes because he *did* get me good. I practically blew a heart valve. While my mind argues back and forth, I choose a safe non-confrontational option.

"Where are we?" I ask calmly. "How much further is Vegas?"

Roy has booked us into a luxury suite on the top floor of the Venetian, a fabulously decadent room with a magnificent view of the Strip.

"Rule number one," Roy says, throwing his suitcase on the bed "on arrival in Vegas, it's Wild Turkey time."

That's a rule? What is this, heaven?

Roy orders two shots of Wild Turkey and we slam them back, both of us grimacing from the after-burn.

"Rule number two in Vegas," Roy shouts happily, "…there are no rules."

Oh splendiferous gods, thank you. I'm close to paradise.

Gazing out at the dazzling wattage that illuminates the Strip, I note a shimmering pool below us.

"Would you like to go for a swim?" I ask Roy.

"Hell no," he splutters. "I'm going to play a few hands."

A momentary flash of disappointment ripples through me, but I dismiss it. Roy doesn't like to swim—so what? I love it. I suit up and head for the pool, and what a pool it is. A huge inviting expanse surrounded by empty chaise lounges. I'm pretty much the only person at the pool because it's 9 p.m. and all the good citizens of Las Vegas are busy smoking, gambling, snorting, drinking and making whoopee. In other words, they're blowing smoke, blowing their money, doing blow, blowing their minds, visiting blow-hoes and blowing off sperm.

Las Vegas blows, baby.

Several lengths underwater cool me to the perfect temperature and once I climb out, there's no need to towel off. Hot wind gusts against my skin as if a giant hair dryer is on, and I feel like God himself is gently blow-drying me. Flopping onto my back I stare up at the stars and feel weepy at the wonder of it all. Life is beautiful. I feel exceedingly lucky to be in this very moment.

Amazingly, the moment actually amps up, because somewhere nearby, the Pointer Sisters must have just stepped on stage. Amidst cheers and applause, their soulful voices drift across the pool "...and when we kiss, ooh ooh…fire".

It's fantastic. My face goes slaphappy on me. I can't smile any wider. Then, as if the universe is pulling out all the stops, fireworks erupt above the hotel. The night sky fills with sparkling intensity. This is stupendous. My whole being lights up.

Staring up at the luminous night sky, I realize that Roy and I will be spending the night on the top floor, in that penthouse suite, entwined together in luxury, with a view of this magical Vegas night. How fantastically, brilliantly un-fucking-believable. I doubt I can get any higher. Compadres, I've hit the zenith. I'm high as a kite on life and drunk as a lord on love. This is beyond paradise. This is nirvana.

As if on cue, the Pointer gals belt out: "I'm so excited and I just can't hide it. I'm about to lose control and I think I like it."

    Yes! Sing it sisters.

Roy is an insatiable gambler. He can "rodeo" for hours burning through his cash, sucking on his Marlboro lights, gulping down Wild Turkey. Does this hoist a red flag for me? Hell no. I love him for it. Go Roy, go! This no-holds-barred behavior is right up my ally. What an extraordinarily exciting guy. Yes, I'm glad *you* can see where this is headed, but since I'm all for my adrenal glands dumping large doses of whoop-de-woo adrenaline into my bloodstream, I find his gambling/drinking/smoking/excessive nature exhilarating. I'm right there with him. I inhale and imbibe with fervor, roaming the casinos while Roy plays cards, and every now and then I sidle up to a "wheel of fortune" machine that has my name on it. Right, my name is loose slot.

    Because I'm a rotten, cheap gambler, I sit at the chosen contraption and bet one quarter at a time. To make my quarters give me more bang for my buck, I entertain myself by hitting the spin button with a different part of my body on each spin. For example: I start with my elbow, then I might use my forehead, maybe thereafter my nose, or possibly my chin. Each breast warrants its own spin. Right mammary gland, left mammary gland. It amuses me, and yes, I'm not totally sober at this point.

    My gambling methods amuse a drunken lady seated next to me, too. She gets in the spirit of things and soon copies every move I make. She is laughing. I am laughing. I run out of upper body parts, compelling me to whip off a shoe and hit the spin button with my big toe. Good thing I'm limber, I knew my yoga practice would pay off. The lady next to me is enthused and willing, but sadly, not quite as limber. She hoists her foot, leans back and, for a second, her stool balance-wobbles then crashes over backwards and she thuds to the floor. We both howl with laughter. The security officer, however, doesn't find our antics quite as humorous—this much fun is not allowed. I'm given a "friendly" warning, which prompts me to ditch my newfound companion, because obviously, she's a bad influence on me.

I head back to find Roy, and babbling away, I describe for him how entertaining and hilarious I am. Astoundingly enough, he is disinterested in my capers and remains solidly focused on his gambling. Again, I don't care. I'm in Vegas having a blast with the man I love. What could be better?

We drink/smoke/gamble until roughly 3 a.m. and then fumble our way back to the hotel room. I'm nervous because I figure we're going to perform the deed tonight, and I haven't had sex in a long time. We've been dating for about 3 weeks now — and we are both ready.

Being drunk helps. I'm relaxed and uninhibited. So is he. It's not the best sex I've ever had, but at least it isn't awful. Thank God, because awful sex is a deal breaker. No matter how much you love someone, if the sex is painful, awkward, or unenjoyable, then the relationship is doomed.

I know — it's like I'm a goddam relationship guru.

Our "honeymoon" night at the Venetian Hotel is followed by a second night at the Rio Hotel. Roy gets a complimentary room at the Rio Hotel due to him squandering shitloads at their casino. Once more, we party hard and stay out drinking and gambling until about 3am. This time, back in the room, we order room service. Roy wants an omelet and that sounds like a damn fine idea. While we wait for our egg-dish delight, Roy flicks on the TV and there's the president, George Bush, in the midst of a speech. My good humor quivers slightly because I detest George Bush.

"What a buffoon," I say haughtily. "I can't stand that man."

Well, apparently Roy feels differently. In fact, he about has a conniption fit. He yells at me how *he* likes the president and what do *I* know, being a foreigner and all, and then unbelievably, he ends his tirade with "why don't you go back to your own country?"

At first I think he is joking. He must be joking, I mean, anyone with a brain can see that Bush is some sort of puppet monkey, right?

Wrong. I'm so wrong. In fact, George Bush gets voted in for a second term, that's how wrong I am.

Roy has a fierce thing going on with his face as he reiterates his sentiment: "You should go back to your own country."

What? You mean South Africa, where I grew up? Or perhaps Scotland, where I was born? Or Germany, where I've spent oodles of time, seeing as my mother is German? Come on, Roy. I had a Scottish father who was raised in Singapore and a Swiss stepfather who moved us all over Africa from Sierra Leon to Namibia to South Africa. I'm not 100 % sure where my country is, or which nationality my "people" are, and I prefer to think of myself as a citizen of Planet Earth. I've been in America for 11 years now, I call it home, and the reason I dislike Bush is that I'm worried he's botching up my adopted home — a home that's been adopted by almost everyone living here in this self-proclaimed melting pot. As the third largest country in the world with a population of more than 315 million, the United States is the most culturally diverse country in the world. Yet, Roy seems to think I should leave America because I don't like George Bush and am voicing it in Las Vegas at 3 a.m. after a drunken night out. Really? Hmm, well shit man — slap me in the face with a wet trout, why don't you? Needless to say, the omelet is eaten in awkward silence and there is nothing sexy happening tonight.

The next day, there are apologies from both sides. Sober, we are both sorry to have had words with one another. I brush it all aside as a drunken misunderstanding because I'm sooo not willing to remove my love-colored lenses and acknowledge what I'm truly up against.

Perhaps this is the point where I should tell you that Roy is a Mormon. Uh-huh. A fully-fledged Mormon, who grew up in the church. A fully-fledged Mormon who did two years of mission work to spread the word (which word I don't quite know — *repressed* perhaps?) A Mormon, who as a 23-year-old virgin, married a similar 23-year-old Mormon virgin, and they then proceeded to do the marriage underpants thing. The sacred Mormon underpants — no, I'm not making this up (yup, get your Google machine out.)

"I'm a Jack Mormon now," Roy explains as if this solves everything.

Uh…okay. Apparently, Jack Mormons can indulge in activities discouraged by the church, such as drinking alcohol, smoking, and premarital sex. They still believe in the Mormon faith but don't attend church on a regular basis, only when they feel like it. Sort of like "Christmas Christians" or "Yom Kippur Jews".

I'm still too unaware of the "Great American Divide" to grasp the major impact that different religious and political views can expound. Therefore, I don't fully understand the fundamental differences between Roy and myself. I naively presume that love will guide us through our cultural, religious and political differences, and conquer all. Yes, I'm an idiot…and I can hear you laughing at me from here.

By the time we get back to my mobile home, the ugly side of our trip is forgotten. All I want is to see Roy as often, and as soon, as humanly possible. I'm like Sara, the autistic advanced reader who can recognize and pronounce all the words but has no idea what they mean. I can see/hear/feel all the red flags waving furiously, and yet can't compute the whole picture that is staring me squarely in the face.

CHAPTER 11

Drugs, Psychopaths and Penis Issues

Diagnosed with Unspecified Mood Disorder, thirteen-year-old Rachel enters the shelter following a suicide attempt where she tried to hang herself with a series of belts strung together. She has also been cutting herself on her thighs and her arms. Rachel is reporting increased mood instability and panic attacks due to parent/child conflict in the home. Just another unloved, unhappy child.

"Can you please clear the table, Rachel?" I ask her after lunch. She simply stares at the ground and appears unwilling to comply.

The Roy confrontation has left me in no state of mind to argue with anyone. I clear the table myself.

"Would you like to share your answers with us?" I ask Rachel during anger management group. Again she stares at the floor and doesn't respond.

Pretty much everything I ask of her, Rachel refuses. She won't participate in any of the groups, or activities, and I find myself becoming more and more annoyed by her mulish refusal to even try. Is she messing with me? Does she do this with all staff members? Am I being overly sensitive because of the flare up with Roy?

On reading the logbook, I find my answer. This small, thirteen-year-old girl is on 600mg of Seroquel — 300mg in the morning and 300mg at night. That's enough medication to sink the Titanic. No wonder she has no motivation to do anything. She's struggling just to walk and talk.

I fight the urge to expound my views to the rest of the staff about how criminal I find this unrestricted handing out of drugs by the medical profession. A thirteen-year-old brain hasn't finished forming yet. How do we know what long-term effects throwing all those chemicals in there will have?

I view Rachel in a whole new light. Of course, now that I realize she is *zonked*, I can totally recognize it. She's got that flat affect reaction to everything. She's zoned out. Damn those shameless pharmaceutical companies and the bastard doctors who prescribe their expensive toxins. Suddenly, I'm all fired up about Rachel's meds — because, you know, Roy told me that I should leave America and go home. There's an uncanny form of supplanting going on in my brain where, since I don't want to think about Roy's behavior towards me, I'll focus my energy on getting Rachel's meds lowered instead.

Look, I understand that there are those who really do need to be medicated (including myself on occasion). For a period, we had Vince residing under our roof, and he was pretty damn scary. This 12-year-old kid had set fire to a trailer in his mobile home park at age 8, killed a rabbit at age 10 and at age 11 had poured some "non-specific" cleaning detergent into his younger brother's soda in the hopes of poisoning him.

Vince had zero empathy, evidenced in his deadpan face. No smile, no frown, not even a look of surprise. The only expression I got to witness on Vince was an eerie smirk that surfaced when he felt he had outwitted the other residents. Though tiny for his age, Vince scared the bejesus out of me. This was a future serial killer. This was a future bad, bad man. What the hell were we meant to do to help this young lad?

Termed a "failure to thrive" baby, Vince was born addicted to meth due to his delightful meth-head mother being unable to control her drug use during her pregnancy. Okay, I realize that obviously it's hard to "control" a drug addiction, but then why have a child? Why keep on having children like Vince's mother did? I don't mind you fucking yourself up, but I'm outraged at you fucking up a defenseless baby.

Vince spent his first three years on earth with his mom in a meth house exposed to all kinds of horrendous stuff. Child Services found

Vince and his two younger siblings huddled around a can of beans, eating out of it with their hands like little feral creatures, all three kids wearing nothing but soiled diapers. Vince was abused, neglected, violated, starved, you name it, and the result was that he shut down until he could no longer feel anything—for himself, or for anyone else (at least that is my take on it). Having only received grossly negligent care, Vince had been unable to form a healthy emotional bond or attachment with his primary caregiver (his mother) during his crucial formative years.

On top of this, there is the theory that kids who suffer in utero drug exposure are born without a conscience. It's their altered brain chemistry. How bizarre is that? To think that it is all a chemical wonder, how we view the world, how we react to the world, how we interact with others. And for me, I think that if a mother ingests heavy drugs or drinks non-stop during pregnancy, she may as well take a bat to her newborn and bash it thoroughly, because drug/alcohol use during pregnancy does just as much damage. I've seen it. Kids with learning disorders, speech impediments, difficulty with self-regulation, physical issues like cleft palates, weak lungs, and stunted growth.

Sadly, Vince's short history is one of prenatal drug exposure combined with malnutrition, physical, sexual and emotional abuse, neglect, deprivation and periods of abandonment. This unfortunate amalgamation certainly increased his risk of developing antisocial symptoms. Extensive abuse and neglect combined with a limited bond to a caregiver is the perfect breeding ground for sociopathic tendencies, and I for one, am not so down with sociopaths.

You can't teach someone to have a conscience.

Having worked at the shelter for eons (or at least it feels that way), I've seen several severely damaged children behave like mini-demons. What the ding-dang-dong are we supposed to do with them?...is all I can think. They are violent, show no remorse or guilt, lack empathy, are manipulative, are punishment insensitive and basically, they don't care. Well, stab me in the neck with a pair of scissors, especially if you're a psychopath.

Psychopaths are not fun—no, not even in Newport Beach. Take the case of Skylar Deleon in Newport Beach who scammed a couple into taking their yacht for a test run out on the ocean, saying he wanted to buy their boat. The couple, Thomas and Jackie Hawks, trusted Skylar because he was shrewd enough to bring along his young, pregnant wife to set them at ease. Once out on the open seas, Skylar forced Thomas and Jackie to sign over the title deed of their yacht to him, then he tied them up and strapped the anchor of the boat to them. At this point Thomas and Jackie begged for their lives, saying: "please, we just want to see our grandchildren again."

Alas, as we know, psychopaths are low on empathy, so Skylar simply tossed them overboard. Apparently, the husband looked at his wife and said: "At least we will be together."

Doesn't that simply break your heart?

In an interview with ABC News (Feb 2009), Skylar stated, "I've never really felt evil. I felt more of…I don't care. I don't care about my life. I don't care about what happens to you."

And there you have it. No remorse, no regret, no emotion. If you aren't shown any love as a child, you don't learn to love. Instead you learn to not love—to not love yourself, and to not love anyone else. Human life has little value for a psychopath.

Later, Skylar claimed he was going to use the money from the boat sale to pay for a sex change for himself. He even went so far as to try and sever his penis with a knife while awaiting trial.

Killing elderly couples and hacking at your penis is not normal behavior. Ergo, good people, let's love all over our children, in case— just saying.

Talking of male organs, I'm going to segue to a "not normal penis" incident, I have with Roy. It's 4th of July and we decide to go wine tasting in the Solvang area. It's my first wine tasting experience ever and I'm instantly an avid fan. Go from place to place and drink? Why, yes please.

We book into a windmill themed hotel because Solvang has this Danish motif going on and evidently Danes are down with windmills.

Er det sandt? Oh ja!

Once we're finished with our wine tasting for the day, we head back to our hotel room and progress from wine to harder stuff, meaning I'm now slugging back Jägermeister shots.

Outside our windmill hotel room, we sit smoking and drinking and shooting the breeze. I'm not sure how we hit upon the subject, but suddenly Roy asks me if I think his apparatus is small. By now I'm too drunk to realize that this is *not* a question I should answer honestly. Since Roy's apparatus is a bit on the reduced side, I try to elucidate for him how that is a good thing for me. I find myself telling Roy about an ex-boyfriend with whom I broke up basically because his penis was too large. I mean had the guy used a "not too deep donut", we may have worked things out. But he didn't, mainly because neither of us knew such a thing existed. Wait, what's that? You don't know about it either? It's a donut shaped ring that the guy places at the base of his penis to prevent him from thrusting all the way in. Yes, of course, absolutely, Google it. And please feel free to use whichever search engine you like—I'm not being paid by Google.

Okay, so naturally the aim of my story is to make Roy feel better about the size of his penis. I guess size *does* matter, but since I'm not a huge girl, in my case "smaller" totally works in Roy's favor. Big is not always a turn on, sometimes it is purely painful. I clarify that I am most satisfied with Roy's manly equipment, no matter the size.

Roy doesn't quite interpret the information in the complimentary fashion I intend it. All he seems to hear is that I had a boyfriend with a monster penis. Face tight, and without a word, he withdraws to the bedroom, climbs into bed and turns off all the lights, leaving me to bump into windmill blades and suchlike in the dark.

"But his penis was too big," I try to explain into the gloom once I find my way inside.

Silence.

"I like your penis. Your small size is much better."

Extreme silence.

"I'm only trying to make you feel better about the size of your penis."

Chasm of silence.

I crawl into bed bereft. I've upset Roy and I've no idea how to take my exceedingly large foot out of my mouth.

Punishing silence emanates forcefully from Roy while I lie crestfallen beside him. Finally, he spits out his revenge. "Playing music in bars is sort of like being a prostitute, don't you think?" he says. "I can't believe that you really enjoy what you do."

Wow.

He finishes up with a grand slam: "I'd never marry someone that sings in bars." With that he turns his back to me.

Tears instantly erupt, and my stomach involuntarily tightens into a nauseating knot. I feel air literally squeeze out of me. That one stung. I presume it was meant to. Shit. Clearly I'm not good enough for Roy. He has no intention of marrying me. Sadly, I'll never get to wear the sacred underwear (did you look it up?)

The Solvang weekend leaves me shaken. I desperately want to be good enough for Roy. Des-per-ately. I'm so desperate that I lose myself completely. I overlook the fact that Roy always makes me come to his place even though I have Samantha at my place. He stops coming to my mobile home altogether, and I make excuses for him: his house is nicer, he doesn't want to bond with Samantha until he's sure we're going to be together long term, he doesn't want to leave his dog alone at home. That's right, his dog outranks my daughter – and I'm fine with leaving my child alone at night to be with Roy. I'm a disgrace.

It's lunacy. I'm addicted to Roy. The dopamine high that he ignites in my tofu-like brain matter leaves me urgently, frantically, frenziedly needing to be with him. I find myself driving back and forth from his apartment to my mobile home sometimes twice a day, even though I utterly hate spending money on gas. Yeah, I don't want to drive Samantha's friends home, or even drive Samantha to school for that matter, but I zoom off to Roy the minute he beckons.

Sorry, Samantha. I have completely lost my footing.

CHAPTER 12

Side Effects Included

It is amazing to me that I work at a youth shelter where my job is to advise struggling teenagers on how to cope with their problems. What a joke. I'm barely treading water myself. I was verging on desperate before I met Roy, but at least my heart wasn't fully exposed as it is now. Now, I'm witlessly deep in wanting, longing, needing, desiring, and my desperation takes on a new dimension.

It's Tuesday and time for more Staph Infection. I'm tense and aggressive and choose this moment to go to bat for Rachel. I vent in staff meeting, which, as I've mentioned, is not really encouraged. But I *need* to blow off steam because my "love" life is transforming me into a big huffy venting machine.

And off I go: "What about Rachel? This kid can't be on such high doses of Seroquel. It's turning her into a zombie. Come on therapists, do something. Make calls. Trot along on your high heels and DO SOMETHING." Of course, I don't say that last part out loud. I simply glare major stink eye at the therapists.

Perhaps it's because I feel so powerless in my home life situation that I overreact at work? Maybe I think that if I can get the therapists to cut Rachel's medication in half, then I'll have accomplished something worthwhile? Something positive? A victory of sorts?

Life just doesn't seem fair at the moment. Not for me, not for Samantha, not for Rachel, not for all the teens at the shelter—and suddenly, I am outraged that the shelter kids are so overmedicated. It seems bloody criminal the amounts of drugs prescribed to these youngsters. Who are these douchebag psychiatrists that are fine with feeding chemicals into a youth's fragile systems, all the while labeling the kid with some lame diagnosis in order to make sure his/her ass is covered. Right, because Doc can't prescribe you Ritalin if you have no disorder, but if you're diagnosed with ADD, then Yahtzee!

The diagnosis of Depressive disorder—NOS (not otherwise specified) seems to be a firm favorite. I'm sorry, but don't we all have that? There are plenty of days (even without a hangover) where I can claim a depressive disorder not otherwise specified.

Then there's Oppositional Defiant Disorder (ODD). That disorder I can undoubtedly assign to myself.

Oh you don't think so? Go fuck yourself!

See what I mean?

And my favorite: Intermittent Explosive disorder (IED). I get that one fairly prominently whenever I climb behind a steering wheel. I can be wonderfully calm and serene until some bastard cuts in front of me. Then I'm Intermittently Exploding all over the show.

Who the fuck taught you to drive, Cocksucker?

This must surely ring a bell for some of you? Right? So, what the hell?

Look, if your parents injected heroin, smoked meth, snorted cocaine, touched you inappropriately, and bounced in and out of prison, don't you think you'd be a tad reactive yourself? Wouldn't you have the urge to intermittently explode? If the kid just sat back and smiled and said, 'mom, dad, just letting you know, everything is hunky dory', now *that* would be worth a diagnosis. That one could be called NRTS—No Response to Shit. It's hugely unfair that a kid who reacts normally to abnormal parenting gets labeled with a disorder. Let's label the parents instead. How about IPD—Inept Parenting Disorder? That way we can report: child reacting within normal range to IPD.

What a messed-up system.

It's not the just the kids at the shelter that are being damaged by pharmaceutical greed. Young Brookie has had to deal with the side effects of Accutane, a medication supposed to help clear up teenage acne. Roche Pharmaceuticals (with total assets over $50 billion, just so you know) released and marketed the hell out of Accutane, and it quickly became a best-selling prescription drug. However, one of the ingredients found in Accutane, called Isotretinoin, was a bit of a problem. Sure, Accutane worked. It cleared up your skin. But if you read the small print, you'd have seen listed amongst the other side effects that Accutane could cause ulcerative colitis.

Um Roche? Could you print that in a slightly larger font please because that is quite a side effect? I mean, ulcerative colitis lasts for the rest of your life, and though your skin may be sparkly-pretty, your poor anus is exploding.

Once Roche found itself defending thousands of lawsuits pertaining to Accutane, it was discontinued. Sadly, not soon enough to save Brookie, who took it for six months, then followed up with the recommended second round for another six months. It was during her second round that she developed ulcerative colitis, which is a debilitating condition. The poor girl has about 5 seconds of lead-time to get to a bathroom. This means that Brooke has pooped in her bed, on her couch, in the car, in my driveway, on her patio…etc. Having colitis makes her nervous to go to school in case she won't make it to the bathroom on time. It makes her nervous to go to a movie in case she can't make it to the bathroom in time. It makes her nervous to have sleepovers, to go swimming, or to eat in restaurants. It's a constant worry for the poor girl. Plus, she has to be vigilant about what she eats because certain foods inflame her colitis and will have her pooping out blood and mucus. Emotional upsets further exacerbate ulcerative colitis, causing it to flare up. And seriously, who can stop being emotional when they're pooping their little hearts out several times a day? This lifelong disease limits Brookie's social life and causes her endless humiliation and stress. Thanks, Roche.

Be that as it may, I get the distinct feeling that everyone would prefer me to shut up when I ask about Rachel's Seroquel dosage at staff meeting. This disturbs me on a deep level because aren't we the people who are supposed to make a difference? We could/should do something about the over diagnosing and over medicating of our country's youth. The entire medical profession appears to either be asleep at the wheel, or complicit.

At least I make enough of a stink that Rachel is sent for a re-evaluation with her psychiatrist (and don't even get me started on the bat-shit crazy psychiatrist we have at our disposal), and thankfully, her dosage is lowered.

Excellent—so I was right. And obviously, I *am* awesome.

Now, how do I get Roy to fall insanely in love with me and want to marry me after all?

CHAPTER 13

Love Song

Roy recuperates from his insulted manhood enough to invite me to go away for another casino weekend excursion in Laughlin. Only this time he is going with friends.

"We're leaving on Thursday evening at 6 p.m." he informs me.

"That's Back-to-School night at Samantha's school," I tell him. "I have to attend but it will be over by 8 p.m. Can you wait two hours, so I can come with you?"

"Uh...no." He says. "My friends have to be on the road by 6 p.m."

Why this couple needs to zoom off to Laughlin at exactly 6 p.m. is baffling and Roy doesn't offer any explanation.

"Please? Please can you wait? Is there no wiggle room? Or can we drive separate from them? I'd love to come with." That's a bit of an understatement. There's nothing in the world I'd rather do, even though Laughlin is basically a stink-hole.

"No. I'm leaving with them at 6 p.m." He sounds irritated. I'm irritating him. My heart sinks.

Roy drives off into the sunset leaving me demoralized and despondent in my mobile home, cursing Samantha's school for having a back-to-school night on this day of all days. I feel ludicrously sorry for myself. I've had to go to these bloody Back-to-School nights every year, and each year I hope that the following year, I'll be able to attend with a partner at my side. A partner who cares for Samantha and me above all else. A partner who is as concerned about Samantha's welfare as I am (even though I'm a fairly useless parent at the moment, I'm still unquestionably concerned with Samantha's wellbeing).

All the other parents show up in couples. They look sufficiently happy and suitably concerned about their children. I want that. I want to fit in with these couples who greet each other with a kind of subliminal understanding that they all belong to the same permanently blessed community. I am an outcast. A pitiful, single mother. Oh look, there's Samantha's mother—still alone. I hear she sings in bars. Good Lord, how appalling. No one will ever marry her.

Fuck-shit-damn.

Whether it's their sanctimonious cheerfulness that makes me hate them, or my own ranting mind, I'm not sure. But I hate them. A lot. Wouldn't it be amazing to walk in with a partner? Just once. Even if my partner were a short, close-eyed, balding, smoking, drinking, gambling addict, Jack Mormon.

I resent every moment of the Back-to-School night. I despise Samantha's teachers for talking so much. Why can't they present their curriculum more succinctly? Then this event would be over, and I could rush home to see if Roy's been delayed or has possibly decided to wait for me.

Yeah, right. Dream on, Walter Mitty.

Mind-bogglingly enough, Roy is not waiting for me, but Samantha is. She wants to know all about the night. Which teachers did I like? Did I see the crazy hair on her new English teacher? Did I notice her artwork on the wall in Mrs. K's class? Her enthused barrage of questions helps feed my hungry heart. I'm glad I went to the school night. Roy is an idiot. Why couldn't he wait a few hours? They are going gambling for three nights. Two hours wouldn't have killed him.

I watch TV with Samantha until 10 p.m., then put her to bed and retreat to my room to find solace in playing my guitar. And what happens? Well, naturally, I write a love song for Roy.

Once it is complete, I lie in bed and cry and cry and cry. I'm hurt. I'm hurt because I know I would have waited a lot more than two hours for Roy. I'm hurt because I take this is as a clear sign that I am not that important to Roy. I'm hurt because I would have loved to have taken Roy with me to Back-to-School night to show all those Newport Beach parents that I am capable of "getting me a man".

The next day, I spend the entire day recording my newly born love song aptly entitled "Falling". I layer harmony upon harmony until the song sounds quite beautiful (please forgive me for blowing my own trumpet here), and I'm excited to play it for Roy. Surely this will work? Surely he'll be flattered and amazed at my talent? Yes? Um...please yes?

Roy phones towards the end of the day. He isn't having a great time and is headed back to Orange County. He has rented himself a car, that's how badly he wants to get back home.

I can hardly contain myself. Does this mean he missed me? He didn't enjoy gambling? What? Impossible.

I rush over to his place the minute he is home (bye Samantha), and bid him to come sit in my car with me, which he does. I pop in the CD that I've made for him and hit play.

Roy listens without making a sound. When the song finishes he looks at me with misty eyes.

"That is the most beautiful 'I love you' that anyone has ever said to me," he says, as he grabs me in a bear hug.

I skyrocket into heaven. Well done, me. One million points to me.

"I wish I had waited for you." Roy squeezes my hands. "We would have had a great time together."

Boys and girls, that is all I need to hear. I'm back on top of the world.

Impressing Roy with my musical wizardry makes me feel so darn special that I want to do it again, only this time I plan to perform magic in a domain that carries serious weight for Roy—the kitchen. Roy has mentioned numerous times that he loves the smell of cinnamon rolls. For him, it conjures up pleasurable memories from his childhood of walking into the kitchen after his aunt, or mother, or someone who wasn't male, had been baking—and apparently nothing smells more like "home" than the aroma of freshly baked cinnamon rolls. I can do that. I can whip up some love and warmth in a dough.

They say the way to a man's heart is through his stomach (and silly me, because I've been trying to get there through his penis), but I can make cinnamon rolls, and not the ones that come from a packet with dough already prepared. No, I shall make them from scratch. I shall fill Roy's nostrils with sheer bloody delight.

To help me do this, I enlist Brooke's mother, Arloa, who (like Roy) is a Mormon. In fact, when they met each other, they realized that they were both from the same small town in Idaho—and that Roy had even lived in Arloa's family house when he was a kid. Maybe it was in that very kitchen that Roy smelled his first baked bliss? I think this cinnamon roll thing may have something to do with Mormons, well, and Scandinavians let's be honest, and quite possibly diabetes too, but that's a different story.

I buy the necessary ingredients and Arloa and I get to work on a Saturday morning. I presume it will take about a half hour, possibly an hour. For me, that is already a huge investment of my time in a kitchen. I'm not happy in the kitchen—it is definitely not my area of expertise. My version of cooking is to slap together meals out of whatever lurks in my fridge and cupboards. This means that poor Samantha has eaten her share of unidentifiable slop. I actually quite enjoy my mystery meals but Samantha feels differently.

"Sardines and pasta? Really? You're the worst cook ever."

Arloa has kindly offered to help me make these cinnamon delights and I'd be lost without her guidance. She shows me how to mix the ingredients together, and soon we're kneading a generous glob of stodgy dough. It's not easy. An hour in, I start to regret my decision of making stupid cinnamon buns, and would be happy to toss everything in the trash. However, Arloa is now fully invested and she's gung-ho to have this demon-dough rise into something heavenly. Let me just tell you that the entire process takes us roughly six hours. I'm beside myself at the end of this crazy, long, boring, preposterous process, and

I can't, for the life of me, understand why anyone would go to such lengths to make something as pointless as cinnamon rolls.

When the glutinous offenders finally come out of the oven smelling pretty much like cinnamon rolls, I'm so peeved, that I don't even try one. Hell no. I loathe those senseless, sugared-up, shit squares with a passion. In addition, I feel unreasonably resentful towards the poor woman whose only crime has been to try and help me ensnare my little Mormon. I bite my lip to avoid being rude to Arloa. It isn't her fault that I'm cranky, and that any good humor I had, has been baked away. What kitchen hell is this? I can't wait to escape. I've been imprisoned for hours, trapped by my own promise to make worthless cinnamon rolls.

Well, forget it. Roy's nostrils can rot in hell.

CHAPTER 14

Vulnerable

Rocking the boat is not encouraged at the shelter. Why? Because we must present ourselves as a well-oiled machine at all times. Even when things go askew, the tendency is to brush everything under the carpet, smile, and move right along. This means that the same problems crop up time and again: keep the logs short, don't wear inappropriate clothing, keep the place clean, no hats allowed in the house. I watch the shelter go round and round in circles, the same old, same old, year in and year out. It makes me feel trapped and depressed. In my dissatisfied state, I fantasize about launching verbal machine gun fire at the entire staff. First, I'd like to snap a round at the therapist who wears low necklines and silly high heels to conduct therapy sessions with our young, hormone-fueled boys.

"Girlfriend!" I'd say. "This is a shelter, not a goddamn hoochie-mama fashion show. Put some suitable clothes on."

Then, I'd have a go at the director. "Other girlfriend!" I'd say, "don't let newbies work a shift together. Okay? Let's have at least one member on staff who knows what the hell they are doing." (Like me for example).

Of course, I don't say a word because honestly, Colleen is a total sweetheart who gives her all to the demanding and endless job that is the shelter director. Plus, nothing I say makes a huge difference...God knows I've pretended to try. On top of that, our staff turnover is fairly high, meaning sometimes the only people we have available to work a shift *are* the newbies. So nothing much changes and we sweep, sweep, sweep our problems under the carpet.

I feel that it's our inept "we do nothing wrong" approach that sees us in sad water one day. It happens during staff meeting with a timid client named Abigail. This dark-haired girl with soft, brown eyes and silky eyelashes, has a bare whisper of a voice that makes it seem agonizingly difficult for her to read her "This is Me" paper to us.

"My name is Abigail. I'm fourteen years old. I live with my mother and father, my twin sister and older brother, my aunt and uncle and three younger cousins. There are ten of us living in an apartment."

Staff lean forward straining to catch what this fragile, young client is saying.

"The reason I came to the shelter is because I tried to kill myself. I...uh...I drank some toilet cleaner. It damaged part of my esophagus."

That's a serious attempt, but luckily, Abigail only swallowed a small amount before her cousin stopped her.

"I am most proud of myself for being alive, and when I leave the shelter I hope to have a reason to stay alive."

Diagnosed with major depressive disorder, Abigail was admitted to the shelter following her seventh suicide attempt. She suffers with chronic suicidal ideation and has been exhibiting isolating behavior, crying, apathy, poor appetite, and low self-worth.

No one really knows what is going on with her because Abigail doesn't talk. She doesn't talk to anyone in her large extended family and she isn't able to open up to anyone of our staff members either. During her one-on-one sessions with her therapist, she simply sits quietly, and politely gives surface answers to all questions. Abigail is keeping everything locked deep inside. Perhaps there is no one she feels safe enough with to share her dark secrets? Not her family, not her friends, not us trained professionals (yes, I use that term loosely). The shelter therapist has been encouraging Abigail to do just that—to share, to open up and allow someone to help her. But each session is like pulling teeth, with Abigail in stalwart silence, too uncomfortable and too mistrusting to open up.

Abigail is what I imagine teenage angels in heaven are like. She never complains. She does all her chores. She is patient, quiet, and polite. Plus, she's beautiful, with deep-set eyes and graceful bone structure. You can't help but want to protect her. Everyone on staff loves her and she seems to love us all right back. On the occasion that she does talk, it's to voice how peaceful and safe she feels at the shelter. She shyly confesses that she'd like to stay at the shelter forever.

Near the end of her stay, Abigail tells her therapist that she has written a letter and would like to read it aloud for everyone at her final staff meeting. The therapist is thrilled that Abigail is feeling confident enough to read aloud, and assumes this is a letter of appreciation for staff, a farewell note of sorts. Lots of clients express their thanks on their last day. They write us little thank you cards, read us poems inspired by their stay, share a dance or song they have practiced. It's pretty frickin adorable and majorly heartwarming.

Tuesday afternoon at 2 p.m., everyone's attention is on Abigail as she stands up to read her "goodbye" letter. Her shiny black hair is braided and purposefully placed over her shoulder, so she can twirl the end of the braid in her nervous fingers. She starts reading in her soft voice and we all pay attention, eager to hear what this reticent girl (that we've all grown to like so much) has to say to us.

"When I was little my dad beat me a lot." Abigail's voice trembles slightly. "I didn't mind the beatings as much as when he started to make me get undressed for him. He made my sister watch while he did things to me, but he never did those things to her."

Staff sits in a dazed silence.

A small choke of dismay escapes Abigail as she continues. "My sister blames me for it. She thinks I must have done something to make my father behave like that towards me because he has never behaved like that towards her."

Her whole being quivers with the effort it takes her to reveal this story. Her body posture screams out her discomfort, yet she persists, determined to share. Possibly she's determined because we've been asking her to open up and share the entire time she's been with us? Perhaps she wants to please us before she leaves? Possibly she is of the understanding that voicing her secret will help her heal?

She stares despondently at the floor and says quietly, "We're twins so we were very close. She used to be my best friend but ever since my father started doing ugly things to me, she treats me like dirt. She hates me." Abigail is clearly heart-broken by her twin sister's rejection.

By now, I'm struggling to hold back my tears. It's not just the wretched information that Abigail is sharing, it's the wounded look on her face, the tremble in her voice, the way her delicate body is curving into itself in an attempt to avoid us, them, everything. Abigail is truly suffering by verbalizing her secrets aloud. We are witnessing a torturous reveal.

I wonder why her therapist isn't jumping in to salvage the situation? Why are we all sitting mutely as this young girl rips herself wide open and shows us her raw bleeding heart?

This is where I feel we let Abigail down. No one says a word. I think we're all a little shell-shocked that this timid girl who has hardly uttered a word during her entire stay now chooses to read this uncensored letter aloud at a staff meeting in front of about twenty of us. Perhaps staff presume (like I do) that Abigail must have cleared this letter with her therapist, because surely no therapist would think it a good idea to go from "not sharing anything" to "exposing your most vulnerable self" in front of a room full of people, even if we are kind, understanding people.

Abigail's letter reading is excruciating, almost too painful to watch. I want to wrap myself around her, and protect her from this "emotional stripping in public." I'm outraged that her therapist isn't stepping in. I'm disappointed in myself for not taking the initiative to do something, anything, to rescue her. But mostly, I am in total awe of Abigail—what a brave girl. What an act of vulnerability. What trust she must have in us. I am truly moved.

CHAPTER 15

Don't Lift the Carpet

It's not long before Roy wants, or more accurately, *needs* to go gambling again, and away we zoom to Pechanga Resort Casino. I'm determined to make everything go perfectly. He won't want to leave early this time, no, because he'll be with moi. He will enjoy himself immensely. His comment of never marrying someone that sings in bars is swept out of my conscious mind and placed under the carpet—shelter style. He didn't mean it. He was hurt by the penis conversation. He *does* want to marry someone like me. I hope.

Roy hits the casino floor the minute we arrive but I take a moment to sit in our room on the 11th floor to soak in a panoramic view of Temecula. I'm filled with excitement, joy, love. So much so, that I have to let out my jubilation somehow or I may platz. I scribble on some scrap paper (that I later transfer to my journal):

August 9th—*Diary Entry*
I'm sitting in Room 11143 in Pechanga, Temecula. There's a view of the rocky hillside and the pool below. The sun is almost set behind the hills, and there's a bleak glow in the sky, which reminds me of England, or winter. Even the car park is worth looking at. I think it's because I am in love. I am so in love. I had no idea I could be this in love. Roy Hoffman! Thank you, God. I never thought I could be this happy. I am completely happy, completely at peace.

Just so you know, I'm not especially fond of England, or winter, or parking lots for that matter, which makes this note all the clearer in its rendering of how blindly in love I am.

We don't fight the entire Pechanga stay, mainly because I keep my mouth extremely shut. I ain't gonna rock this little miracle rescue boat, no sir. I'm starting to understand the director at the shelter. It's a quiet desperation that keeps her silently smiling and pretending everything is super-duper, while her insides scream: Don't lift up the carpet! Don't lift up the carpet!

Roy and I return to Pechanga a few weeks later, and again I write about it.

August 30th — *Diary Entry*
I'm sitting in Room 11244 this time. No view of the pool, only mountains and construction — not that spiffy. Anyhoo, I'm still madly in love with Roy Hoffman and when I say madly, I mean it's incredible. He is amazing to be with. My brain is sooooo happy to meet another similar brain to talk to. I can't believe how starved I've been for companionship. I am astonishingly happy to be with him. He is trustworthy, honest and commits 100%

No matter how astonishingly happy I am, Roy is not that trustworthy, or that honest, and sadly, his method of making sure he doesn't have to commit 100% (to me at least), is to slowly force me into a dark hole. He does this by a gradual condemning of me. It happens progressively over the following weeks as everything about me comes under close examination.

It starts with a simple: "What is that black thing on your chest? Is that a mole? That's kinda gross. You should get that looked at."

His remark has me scrutinizing my skin and wishing I were smooth as a jellybean. A mole that I've had for years, that has never worried me before, suddenly feels colossal. I rush to cover it up as best I can. Quick side note here: that mole eventually fell off one day after a lengthy jacuzzi. Yeah, what's that about?

Sometimes Roy's criticism appears semi-disguised as a compliment. He taps his front teeth one day and says, "My teeth aren't real. These are veneers. Your teeth are a little yellow. Veneers would look good on you."

That remark whips me into a tooth-polishing frenzy. All I hear is "yellow teeth" and am instantly self-conscious about my not-so pearly whites. How come I've never noticed how discolored my teeth were before?

Roy's remarks seem harmless at first, but they are the beginning of a systematic chipping away of my self-esteem. Turns out, Roy is a meister-criticizer, and I guess I'm an excellent "have your self-esteem chipped away" recipient. My self-esteem wavers, shrinks, dissolves.

Arriving to pick me up to go kayaking one Saturday morning, Roy demands to know why I haven't showered yet.

"But we're going kayaking." I say in my defense. "I'm going to get sweaty and possibly wet. I plan to shower after."

This is not good enough for Roy. He is visibly upset that I haven't "cleaned up" for him, that I'm not minty fresh to greet him. In my mind, I am perfectly presentable, and I'm taken aback by his outburst.

Thing is, I am not "clean" enough for Roy, period. Not in body, not in mind, not in lifestyle. I'm simply not a virtuous virgin.

His criticism goes on and on. My cooking ability sucks (he is right on that one). I look better "gussied up" (he may be right on that one too). So…uh, how often do I shower? (He showers twice a day) Why do I look down on religion? What exactly are my morals? Don't I *want* to be more virtuous? What? Hello? Casino boy?

I should be furious with him, but I'm not. I'm too blissed-out with Roy and remain stubbornly oblivious to all his foibles. I refuse to register that things are amiss, even when Roy has a dinner party at his house and grows increasingly anxious for his guests to leave so that he can mop the floor. At the time, I think: "Aww look. My guy likes to clean. How adorable."

I don't think: "Wow! My guy is a total germaphobe with a touch of the OCD thing going on".

It's clear to me now of course: gamble, gamble, gamble—clean, clean, clean. In other words: sin, sin, sin—atone, atone, atone. But how can I fault him when I'm a walking love disaster? When I'm helpless, hopeless and hapless. I'm ridiculously in love. Annoyingly in love. Pathetically in love.

For me, Roy's voice cuts through everything. It resonates differently from anything else in the world. I can hear him above chatter, music, slot machines, sirens. Like a mother with a newborn child, my ear is instinctively tuned to him, listening. I love to hear his voice. Even if what I hear is criticism. I'm still keen to hear it. In my mind, Roy is my savior. He *is* going to marry me. I will get a green card and so will Samantha. We will move in with him. I won't have to work at the shelter anymore. I can concentrate on my music. Roy will get his movie made. I'll do the music for his film. 'Twill be a blockbuster. Yes, yes, yes.

Roy acknowledges that he's critical of me, but assures me, he is far more critical of himself. He discloses that he has a continuous unappeasable voice in his head, an inner critic that never shuts up. Roy knows that no matter what he achieves in his life, it will never be enough. He will always need to do better. Again, I pay no attention when this is quite obviously a clue to his psychological makeup. He is rigid, critical, sanctimonious, a gambler, a smoker, a heavy drinker, has low self-esteem hidden under a loud personality, and he is sadly verkrampfed in the sexual department—Oh marry me. Marry me!

Yes, yes, of course, Roy is not all bad. He is also funny, entertaining, sexy (at least to me he is), witty, sparkly and very generous. Plus, he *is* clean, and he has a clean two-bedroom apartment that I secretly prefer to my mobile home because it has that wonderful/dreadful thing called air conditioning.

My "trustworthy, committed, honest" boyfriend and I visit one casino after another. I have no problem with this at all. Casinos serve alcohol, allow smoking, and we can stay up all night if we so choose. Pure joy, really.

It's at Mountain High Casino in Black Hawk Mountain, Colorado, that Roy insults me to the edge. We are about 10 months in and I'm still giddy-drunk with love. He books us into a room with not only a gorgeous view, but also a huge jacuzzi bathtub. We soak in the hot bath together, watching snow fall on the mountains outside. It's outrageously fantastic. I'm all steamed up and fully relaxed, when Roy looks between my legs and says: "Eeww, your vagina is purple."

I quickly cover my privates, thinking I'm a hideous shameful monster with disgusting mal-colored parts. I say nothing, but it weighs on me…and weighs on me. The more I think about it, the more it upsets me. Who says "eeww" to their partner's privates? Who attacks you when you're naked and vulnerable? Sticks and stones may break my bones, but words, hell those can smash you to smithereens.

It makes me think about Abigail opening herself wide up during staff meeting. What if we'd said "Eeww—we don't want to hear what your father did to you because it makes us uncomfortable"?

I know that's why Abigail's twin sister lets her horror out on Abigail, because hating on her sister is an easier "solve" than facing the reality that her father (one of her primary care-givers) is a disgusting, depraved douchebag.

Same thing with Roy. Since he is sexually repressed, the sight of my vagina makes him uncomfortable. It's easier to blame the technicolor of my vagina than the lackluster color of his entire religious upbringing.

I should be angry with Roy, but I'm not. I should say something to him, but I don't. Instead, I climb into our hotel bed with full-length pajamas on, and know that even if it gets hot as hell, I will not be taking these PJs off tonight—no sir.

As Roy drifts into slumber land, I lie awake alongside him listening to his shallow snoring, feeling resentful and hurt, and relentlessly overthinking the hue of my vagina. Roy can't hear me and doesn't register it, but I whisper to his sleeping form anyway. "You know what, Roy? Don't insult my vagina, okay? It's unkind and not cool."

Yeah. I sure told him.

Besides, what the hell color should my vagina be? Green? I'd say that dunked in hot water, purple is probably pretty darn normal. Please don't tell me if I'm wrong here. I'm not sure I want to know.

CHAPTER 16

Invisible

I arrive at the shelter in the midst of a hullabaloo. It doesn't matter to me. The minute I walk through the front door, *I* feel safe. This is my sanctuary where nobody cares what color my hoohoo is. This is my "shelter," and I can handle whatever panic is going on inside these walls. It's my own life on the outside that I can't handle. It's my own mounting panic that pounds my heart rate to overload.

Tonight I'm doing a graveyard shift, therefore it's 11 p.m. when I arrive, which means the kids should be sleeping. Five of them are, but a new arrival, a kid that entered the shelter during the afternoon, is escalating into an apparent manic state. He's pacing and jabbering and is unable to respond to staff's request to stay in bed. How can he? He is pumped full of adrenaline and soaring. I think I can relate.

Since this 17-year-old is a 6 foot 2, big, burly lad, the police have been called. When I walk in the front door, staff are waiting for back up to arrive to deal with the young man.

"Don't worry, I'll sit with him," I assure them, and tell them to go ahead and finish up their paperwork and clock out. No problem, happy campers. I can manage anything as long as it isn't tied to my own emotional well-being.

The agitated resident, Dorian, wears dark sunglasses although it is pitch black outside. He tells me he can't take the sunglasses off because the lights are too bright for his eyes.

"They suit you," I tell him, and sit down on the couch.

Staff have put on a movie to try and calm him, but being manic, Dorian has turned on the stereo to blast loud music as well.

"Do you mind if I turn one of these off?" I ask. "There's too much noise going on in here."

Although Dorian's pacing, he's in good humor. "The music helps me relax," he explains, "I've seen this movie, you can turn that off."

I press pause on the film and discreetly lower the volume of the stereo. I'm trying to regulate the atmosphere here, hoping to soothe Dorian. I also unlock the front door, so the police can simply come inside—just in case.

"I can speak 23 languages," Dorian tells me.

"Damn. That's impressive, I can only speak three."

"Yeah, and last time I was in China, I won this watch for skateboarding. Check it out," he shows me a neon-green, plastic watch on his arm. "I'm a champion skateboarder."

I doubt this poor kid has ever been anywhere near China, or that his plastic watch is of any worth, but I know not to refute anything. I simply go with it.

"Awesome, you're a lucky dude."

"Shit man, I'm like a king over there in Tokyo." He grins, unaware that he is now actually big in Japan.

A police car pulls up outside.

"Hey, I see the police are here," I say amicably. "Don't worry, they come by all the time to check on the shelter. They're pretty cool guys."

Dorian sits down on the couch next to me. He doesn't seem upset by a potential police visit, and I'm relieved.

"Come in, door's open," I call out when the police knock on the front door.

I stay put with Dorian on the couch because I imagine that me sitting by him, with my zen-like presence (cough), is helping to keep him calm. Whether this is accurate, or just me thinking way more of my abilities than is actually true, I don't know. Regardless, three policemen enter the living room and the head officer asks Dorian how he's doing.

"Good." Dorian beams at them.

"Can you take your sunglasses off please, son?" the officer squints at Dorian, sizing him up.

"I can't, it's too bright in here. It hurts my eyes."

"Ok. Can you stand up, please?" The officer continues.

"Am I in trouble?" Dorian starts to fidget.

"Can you stand up please, son?"

"I need to get my...my...uh…" Dorian does not stand up. Instead he slides his hands behind him on the couch.

I try to determine what he is reaching for, but I can't see. The police don't know what he's reaching for either.

"Put your hands where I can see them!" the officer immediately commands, placing his own hand on his gun.

Holy, sweet Jesus on a stick. Suddenly I envision this whole scenario going dreadfully wrong.

Dorian still doesn't comply. He keeps groping for something behind him, "I'm just getting my...my...what's it called again?"

I soundlessly start sliding away from him, fearing the worst. Calm presence be damned. I don't want to be in range if there is a trigger-happy moment here.

"I said, put your hands where I can see them!" the officer barks—no more mister nice guy.

"I just want to put my...my sweater on. Geez." Dorian says, getting visibly upset.

"Put your hands where I can see them right now!" the officer practically yells, and I prepare to dive for cover.

Fortunately, Dorian brings his hands out from behind him.

"Stand up," the officer orders, and thankfully, Dorian does. Behind him on the couch, wedged between the cushions, is his sweater. He really was reaching for his sweater. As he picks it up, the policeman snatches it away from him and shakes it out.

"You can put your sweater on later." The policeman says sternly. Dorian's quickly bustled out of the shelter into the waiting police car. I wave good-bye to the poor soul, wondering what chance someone like him stands? His brain chemistry is all messed up, and though he's only 17, he's huge and appears threatening even when he isn't.

In the staff office, I read the notes on Dorian. Here is where I find out why he wanted his sweater. Dorian has a diagnosis of bipolar disorder with psychotic features, and symptoms of a psychotic episode include delusions. In the same way that Dorian believed he was a champion skateboarder in China and could speak twenty-three languages, he also believed that his sweater could make him invisible.

Maybe I should have read the notes first? That would have been helpful.

The next time I go to see Roy, he has some of his friends over and we all play basketball together, or at least a muddled version thereof. My period starts unexpectedly, and I bleed into my pants, leaving me the humiliation of having to ask Roy for something to wear. How about that? I *am* dirty, Roy. Shamefully soiled through.

Soon, I'm wearing a pair of Roy's sweatpants while playing basketball. They're saggy, not flattering at all — so with this bag lady style, and cramps gripping my ovaries, I feel truly unsexy. Still, I make an effort to remain upbeat about playing. Thing is, I'm not the most athletic or coordinated person in the world, and this jumping about in shapeless pants, bloated and ungainly is no fun for me whatsoever. Roy leaps nimbly about the court, and after I miss every ball that he throws my way, he begins to focus solely on Sylvia — a beautiful Spanish girl, who is bubbly, energetic, a good shot and spiffily dressed in cute, well-fitting clothes.

The more Roy focuses on her, the clumsier I become. Down the ugly slope I slither, feeling less and less attractive until I wish that the ground would please open up and swallow me, and my bleeding, purple bajingo.

At this moment, I fully appreciate Dorian's attempt to live in an alternate reality. Wouldn't it be splendidly satisfying to look at Sylvia and say "one of my songs hit number one in China today".

Yes, it would.

Or Dorian's invisible sweater — I could go for a jersey of that particular talent right now.

CHAPTER 17

Break up...Break down

During an afternoon group at the shelter, we watch an hour show on unhealthy relationships. It's an Oprah Winfrey episode about teenage girls in love with young men who, slowly but surely, commandeer the girl's lives. On the show, the girls take turns to disclose their experiences and it's easy to notice that all their stories have a common thread. The boyfriend starts off full of compliments that gradually turn to criticism. As the relationship continues, the boyfriend begins to tell the girl what clothes to wear and how much make up to put on. Then the boyfriend wants to know where the girl is at all times. Soon she has to "report in" through texts or phone calls, or there will be a huge argument that, more often than not, ends up in a physical altercation.

One of our female residents starts to cry. "My boyfriend has treated me in this way," she says mournfully as the information shared on the TV resonates with her. "And he isolates me from my friends."

"I'm so glad you recognize that," I immediately praise her. "How great that you're here at the shelter where you can learn to avoid relationships that hurt you, and instead form healthy relationships that support who you are."

Mother of God, I'm so full of shit. What a fraud I am. I can clearly hear the young girl in me crying, too. My inner child is crying because she knows that if Roy really cared about me, he would stop criticizing me. He would encourage me, not demean me. He would gladly incorporate Samantha in our activities, not isolate me from her. He wouldn't tell me I look better with make-up on, or take me shopping so that I have some "decent" clothes to wear. He wouldn't shame my singing career. And he certainly wouldn't insult my privates. Right?

Still, the warning bell ringing in my head is ultimately not loud enough to stop me from seeing Roy. It would have to be a very loud bell at this point. One that basically rings my head right off my neck and splinters my heart from my brain.

I pat the girl on the back and tell her she doesn't deserve to be treated that way.

I can't stop seeing Roy, quite simply because I love him—and I'm crazed by this love. I'm no longer rational. I am powerless. Does Roy realize he will never meet anyone that loves him as much as I do? I wonder if he has taken this into account? Probably. In fact, he most likely hopes he'll never have someone love him this much ever again, because it is *too* much. I've successfully set Roy on a precariously high pedestal and left him nowhere to venture but off the edge. All he can do is fall off.

It's a Wednesday evening when he decides to take that inevitable plunge, and like the honest, committed, true gentleman that he is, he does it over the phone.

"I'm done." He says.

"Done?" I repeat stupidly.

"Done with trying. This 'us' thing, it's not working."

"Huh?" my brain seizes. My heart seizes. I'm having a fucking seizure. "But we're carving Halloween pumpkins tomorrow." I say, as if carving pumpkins is something that no one in their right mind would miss—ever. "Can we still do that?"

I realize that I sound idiotic, but I can't believe he's breaking up with me. I just can't. It seems impossible, because I love him so much. My brain is shutting down. Code red in my head. System failure.

Had I known the heartache ahead, had I known how long I'd be hooked on Roy's rod (no rudeness intended), had I known that he was going to walk all over me until his heels crunched my face deep into the dirt, perhaps I would have said "shove a pumpkin up your ass you little bastard!"

Ah yes, hindsight—20/20.

Instead, I'm horrendously shortsighted and cling on tightly, terrified to let go.

"Umm, okay." Roy mutters. "That does sound like fun."

I breathe a huge sigh of relief. He is still coming tomorrow, and by then, he'll have changed his mind. He will realize that he is foolish for not wanting to be with me.

Alas, carving pumpkins is not a life altering experience (for anyone, really). I spend the evening with vicious anxiety gnawing on my stomach lining. I stab clumsily at my pumpkin having lost all dexterity and finesse in the carving department. Roy's rejection has left me ham-fisted and panicky.

"Please don't break up with me," I beg him. "Let me try and be better. I'll learn to cook."

I can sense the door closing, and I'm freaking out.

"Look," Roy finally says, "let's take a break and we'll see how we feel in two weeks' time."

Two weeks? That's like a trillion light years away.

"Uh...ok." I reply. "Maybe that's a good idea.

Can someone pass me the razor blades, please?

On returning to my mobile home, Samantha chooses this moment to enlighten me that she intends to pierce her ears for a third time.

"I don't need your permission," she informs me aloofly. "I'm just telling you."

For some reason, her icily delivered newsflash crushes me. It's too much for me to handle. I'm overwhelmed by my ineffectiveness, my pointlessness. I have sunk to the level of a nonentity. My "weigh in" is weightless. I'm impotent and otiose. I don't count. Not in Samantha's eyes, not in Roy's eyes—and these are the two humans that I want to impress most of all. I rush to the bathroom and throw up.

Samantha gets her ears pierced, and I start on my two weeks of yearning, craving, and pining for Roy. I pretend that everything is okay, but underneath my phony bravado, I'm terrified. Towards the end of the two weeks, I meet Shirley at the Quiet Woman in Corona Del Mar (the pick-up joint where I met Roy). Shirley's in top form, chitchatting away, wide-eyed and charming.

"I channel entities," she tells her captivated male audience. "I can sense things. Like if there was something wrong with you, I'd feel it. I'm a complete empath…a psychic empath."

"Is there anything wrong with me?" a nondescript, white-collar guy asks.

Shirley giggles coquettishly, giving him the once over. "Absolutely nothing."

Usually I'd join in the flirting, but my seduction skills are at zero because there *is* something wrong with this guy—he is not Roy.

I step out the back to bum a cigarette and suddenly I spot Roy across the way. My heart lurches at the sight of him and my alcohol intake escalates sharply. I ignore him, and, magically my flirting skills resurface with a bang. I sidle up to the best-looking guy I can find, lean in super close and whisper in his ear, "May I please have a cigarette, and can you pretend that you think I'm amazing because my ex-boyfriend is busy watching, and I'm hoping to make him jealous."

Mr. Handsome winks at me, and whips out a cigarette.

"Here you go, beautiful," he says loudly, throwing his head back and laughing like I'm marvelously hilarious. Mr. Handsome plays this game well. We joke and giggle, and "tête-à-tête" like we were born for each other.

It works. Roy comes over. Nodding at my coconspirator, I turn my attention to Roy, and soon, I've ditched Shirley and am in Roy's car headed back to his house for some serious make up hanky-panky. I'm over the moon. Hooray! I've won Roy back (yes, with my purple vagina). We *are* going to get married. I *am* going to get a green card. *And* Samantha will get a green card. Joy to the world and to any other worlds that may possibly exist, too.

Our happy reunion lasts all of five days, and then, Roy announces once more that he is done. He doesn't want a break—he wants a break up. He uses my handsome coconspirator as proof against me—I am

NOT what he is looking for in a marriage partner. His wife will not be out in bars, bumming cigarettes from strange men. Ay caramba! Shit damn in a big brown bucket.

I fall apart. This break up absolutely breaks me—my ego, my spirit, my heart—kaput. I fear I might die from not seeing Roy. Honestly, I'm not exaggerating. Apparently, the flood of stress hormones that surge through you during a break up can weaken the heart, hence the name "broken heart syndrome." This break up is a trauma to my mind, body and spirit. I'm stunned into an unmitigated void.

I can't believe how painful it is. Why haven't those stupid pharmaceutical companies made a pill for *this* shit? I'd be down with anything that blocked out this pain. Wipe my mind clean, please. Ignorance *is* bliss. Maybe frontal lobotomies can be groovy?

I phone my sister Linda who lives in England. Linda's always been the voice of reason for me. She's my go-to person. She consistently gives me solid, grounded advice that helps me regain my senses. She has my back all the way. Thank God for Boemsie (yes, that's what I call her).

"Boemsie," I sob into the mouthpiece. "Roy has broken up with me."

"Oh no. I'm so sorry to hear that." She knows how smitten I am. I cry soundlessly as grief overpowers me. Linda knows I'm crying.

"Look," she says. "You told me that this chap is rigid and controlling and insults you. He doesn't sound like he deserves you. You're a magical, free spirit, and I think he will only bring you down. You need someone who will allow you to grow, and who will grow with you, not against you. I believe you may have just had a lucky escape."

I love Linda for saying that—a lucky escape. It is not a break up, it's a lucky escape. But at this moment, I don't feel lucky. I feel heart broken.

I head to Mother's Market (as one does when one's heart is broken), and inquire as to what natural remedies they could suggest for ferociously out of control anxiety. A tattooed, beanie-wearing, hipster employee suggests "Holy Basil".

Back in my mobile home I gulp down two capsules of Holy Basil while my heart pounds with inexplicable terror and my mind races round and round in ever decreasing circles. Why doesn't Roy love me? Why doesn't he? Why Roy? Why? Roy! Roy! Roy!

Okay, now here is something somewhat kooky that if anyone out there can explain to me, please do. Within about 20 minutes, I feel an incredible sense of freedom. I feel light as a feather. My heart beats beautifully, and my mind turns calm and clear. Roy is not the one for me. He is too strict and has too many rules that apply not only to me, but to himself as well. He will not change. He will eventually stifle me, suppress my spirit, squash my very being. He will never be supportive, or loving of who I am, or recognize my true essence. My sister is completely right. I have dodged a bullet. I *have* had a lucky escape.

I'm elated and bounce about the kitchen preparing Samantha a fabulous dinner, chatting away with her, feeling more confident than I have in months. Yes-ah! Niki is back. I like Niki. I've missed her. I'm delightfully relieved. I can breathe again. Nice long deep breaths at my own pace.

Halle-fucking-sun-shining-day-lujah.

This Holy Basil is really terrific stuff, except the following day, I wake up with a crushing, dead weight on my chest, and all I want is for Roy to love me again. Any clarity from the previous evening has evaporated, gone, vamoosed, and I'm back to thinking how pathetic and wretched I am. Apparently I'm only funny, clever, attractive and talented if Roy loves me.

Two more capsules of Holy Basil do nothing. I wait an hour and swallow another two. Still nothing. I finish the entire bottle of Holy Basil over the next few days, but the euphoric feeling of freedom never returns. So yeah — what the hell was that? Anyone?

Although Roy has broken up with me, he keeps calling. He keeps inviting me to places. And yes, of course we keep having sex. It's not healthy, and I know it, but as you may have garnered by now, I do whatever Roy wants. Yeah sure, I had a moment of clarity, but that was a million years ago—or it may as well have been.

Christmas arrives and Roy invites Samantha and me to come over to help decorate his Christmas tree. I'm thrilled that he has included Samantha, but she hates the idea. Hard cheese for Samantha, because I basically drag her there against her will.

Roy has gifts for both of us. Samantha gets new clothes and $50 (which she *is* ok with) and I get a new guitar case and $500. It's guilt money for sure, because Roy probably knows that he shouldn't be sleeping with me, and calling me, and keeping me flapping on the end of his incredibly alluring hook. Obviously he enjoys keeping me dangling on this hook, because the words he writes in his Christmas card have me biting down hard on the sharp, pointy end.

Merry Christmas, Nicola May (that's what he likes to call me)
I want you to know that you have been an absolute angel to me. You are without a doubt one of my favorite human beings. You have opened my eyes in so many ways. I am so grateful for all you have shown me. I hope this coming year brings you all the happiness and success you so deserve. I have absolute faith in your many talents—they will pay off. There are very few gorgeous geniuses out there. You are truly one of a kind. I'm forever thankful to know you. I love you very much Niki Smart—huge amounts, Roy

What the hell am I supposed to do with that? How can I walk away from someone who thinks I'm the best thing in the world? I want someone who loves me "very much" as his card says. Why? What? Huh? Arrrggh!

To perplex me further, for some inexplicable reason he sends me yet another Christmas card. Yes two Christmas cards. This next one again brimming with love.

Nicola May
To one of my favorite humans on the planet. A beautiful woman inside and out. A clever witted, sharp-minded, multi-talented singer/songwriter, guitar playing, screenwriting, M&M eating, Boggle playing, Bush hating, pig loving, kind hearted, an absolute one of a kind. No matter what the future holds in store for us, I want you to know, you will never be alone. There will always be a Hoffman out there that loves and cares for you.

¡Qué susto! Roy sees me. He appreciates me. He loves me. He gets who I am. He's thankful to have met me, and to have me in his life. And yet? Hello? WTF? Someone please shoot me.

Once Roy's tree is adorned, we pose in front of its twinkling beauty for a photo op. Samantha snaps a shot of Roy and me—I'm wearing a t-shirt that reflects my special Christmas mood. "F**k Xmas" it says. Roy takes one of Samantha and me. As Samantha throws an arm around my shoulders, she whispers in my ear, "I'm going to try and look as ugly as possible in this photo."

She manages quite nicely. I'd put that photo in here but that doesn't seem fair to Samantha (who is, of course, gorgeous).

Roy drives off to spend Christmas with his family in Wyoming, but before he leaves, he very kindly hands me the key to his shimmery-shiny, crispy-clean condo. His complex has a swimming pool and Roy knows how much I love swimming. (See? He's not all bad.)

Naturally, while I stay at his place, I take the opportunity to sift through every single item that he owns. I scour the place from top to bottom until I find what I'm looking for: photos of ex-girlfriends. These ex-lovers are stored in a cardboard box in the bottom drawer of his office desk. I view the photos like one does an accident. I know I shouldn't look. I know it's going to be nasty, but I *have* to see their faces. I study their expressions like they hold some clue, some answer that I need, need, need. For the majority of the pictures, Roy has his arm around his 'girl-of-the-moment' and a smile on his face, exactly like he does in a dozen photos of us.

And quelle horreur—for most of the girls, there exists a Christmas photo of him and her standing together before a Christmas tree. It's an exact duplicate of the one Roy and I snapped right before he departed for Wyoming. Oh, sick feeling. Sick feeling indeed. I'm going to end up in that box in the drawer. All our lovely photographs, our fun times, our smiling faces banished to the bottom drawer along with all the other ex-wanna-be Mrs. Hoffmans. How horribly horrible.

I no longer want to stay in Roy's apartment. Suddenly I feel like an intruder. I slink back to my mobile home park/prison, and since Samantha is out with her friends, I'm all alone and thoroughly miserable, thank you very much.

Then unexpectedly, Roy calls.

"I miss you," he says. "If I buy you a ticket, will you fly out here and join me for New Year's Eve? Do you want to do that? Then we can drive back to Orange County together."

Do I want to do that? Do I want to do that? Yes, yes, yes, a million times yes.

I'm going to Wyoming.

Fuck you, Holy Basil!

CHAPTER 18

Round Two

I'm on a graveyard shift again, and though the long nights are exhausting, nothing can dampen my mood. Roy has bought me a plane ticket and I'm all set to fly out of John Wayne Airport on the 31st of December courtesy of United Airlines. I am super charged.

Around midnight, the phone rings and I snap it up before Ben can even get to it. This in itself is a miracle, because as you know, I typically avoid answering the shelter phone at all costs.

"County Youth Shelter, Niki speaking," I virtually singsong out. Ben is probably wondering if I've been drinking. No, my lovely little coworker, I'm high on life. Well, more accurately, I'm high on Roy's life…with me in it.

Child services are on the phone, and once again they have Nina and her mother Rowena in their charge.

"Most certainly we have room for an emergency admit," I answer the officer, while Ben eyes me suspiciously. "I'll need to talk to both parent and child, even though they've been through this before."

Soon I'm speaking with Rowena. "Will you be bringing Nina in?" I ask, remembering her fear of driving from the last time.

"No, I can't drive." She says tearfully. "I've taken four different medications and I've been shot."

I presume Rowena means she's been shot with some type of tranquilizer. God knows the poor woman could use it. But on talking with Nina, I realize that what Rowena means is that she's been shot…in the face…by Nina…with a BB Gun. I almost burst out laughing. You can't make this stuff up. It's hilarious, until I think

110

about Samantha blasting me in the face with a BB gun. Yeah again, that's not quite as funny.

"Did you drink wine before you came in to work?" Ben asks, his über-blond eyebrows lifting in such a cute manner that I just want to bite his face off.

"I'm happy, Ben. Happy, happy, happy." I grab him in a bear hug to demonstrate my joy and to radiate my elation all over him.

Ben's not quite as thrilled and quickly squirms free. I bow low in front of him. "And now I'm going to get the bed ready for Nina."

Undoubtedly, I'm resplendent in my hopefulness.

Nina will be rooming with Shondah, a skinny child who has been with us for several weeks. Shondah has overstayed her 32-day limit and we've had to make special provisions to legally lengthen her stay at the shelter. Thing is, Shondah has nowhere to go, and all our teams are scrambling to find a placement for her. She's 15 with the emotional and intellectual level of about a ten-year-old. I know Shondah's history. Her mother abandoned her when she was six, leaving her in the care of her father. Sadly, a few years later, her father was diagnosed with cancer and Shondah has had to watch helplessly as he's deteriorated from walking with a cane, to using a walking frame, to being in a wheelchair, to being bed-ridden attached to an oxygen tank with tubes stuck up his nose to help him breathe.

Unable to deal with the imminent abandonment by her father as well, Shondah built up a rage against him. Fueling her rage was the fact that she has had to help dress him, feed him, move him from one room to the other, and after a few months, Shondah couldn't handle it anymore. Using a razor blade, she cut a hole in his oxygen tube.

"I couldn't take the gurgling noise no more, and the smell… everything," she admits during a group therapy session.

Thankfully, this didn't kill him, but it did hospitalize him and with nowhere to go, Shondah was brought into the shelter. Possibly that is what she wanted all along? Simply to bring an end to her role of nursemaid to her dying father. To find relief from her depressing home life and to gain some nurturing for herself.

I'm halfway up the stairs, going to prepare the bed for Nina, when an acidic stench sears my nostrils. It's not hard to determine that the smell is coming from Shondah's room. Nearing her bed, I can tell it is her urine I'm smelling. It's fiercely strong and reeks of ill health.

Shondah eyes me uncomfortably as I enter the room.

"I've gone and soaked my bed up." She stares miserably out the window. "I don't know why, 'cos I haven't drank water in over two days. I didn't want to wet the bed."

The urine she's been laying in is a dark and smells of ammonia.

"Listen Shondah, you have to drink water. At least four glasses a day, okay?" No wonder her pee smells so bad. This girl hasn't had any water to flush out her system in a couple of days.

"But then I'll wet the bed again." She whimpers unhappily, "and you guys will ask me to leave."

"Absolutely not. No one has ever been sent away for wetting the bed. Come on, let's get you some fresh bedding." I offer her my hand to help tug her up out of the wet mess. "If you're worried about wetting the bed, don't drink anything after 6 p.m., but your body needs water during the day. You're dehydrated and basically peeing out your kidneys. Let's go drink a glass of water right now."

I make her chug a glass of water, and then send her to shower while I strip the bed. I nearly gag on the odor and curse the shelter for the low pay rate. I should get paid handsomely for doing this.

Once both beds are made, I spray Febreze and instantly everything is happy again. Shondah climbs back into bed and I sit with her for a moment.

"There's a new girl coming tonight; she'll be sleeping in here with you, okay?"

Shondah nods and her face lights up. "What's her name?"

"Nina. Let her sleep though. She's going to be tired and probably grumpy. You guys can chat in the morning." I pat Shondah and pull the blankets up around her. "Go back to sleep and don't worry about peeing the bed. It's no big deal. But make sure to drink water—that *is* a big deal. You don't want to damage your body. I'm serious."

Shondah grabs my hand and squeezes it. "Goodnight, Miss Niki." She smiles shyly.

"Goodnight, Miss Shondah." I respond. Low pay be damned—*this* is my recompense.

The ambulance drops Nina off, and once again, she argues that she didn't actually agree to come into the shelter.

"Where would you rather be, Nina?" I ask her.

"Back at the hospital. They don't have as many rules there. There I can swear without having to do a lame consequence. This place is retarded. I hate this place. If I have to stay here, I'll kill myself."

"I'll kill myself" are the magic action words. The kids in the system learn pretty quickly that if they threaten suicide, it shakes things up. People *have* to pay them attention then.

"What can they do for you at the hospital?" I ask. "It won't change anything. At least here we can work on solutions for your family. Your mom can come in and get help. You can get help."

"If I have to stay here, I'll find a way to end my life." Nina sulks hard.

I know she's merely being difficult. I know Nina doesn't really want to harm herself. I also know that she is upset and hurt, and frustrated, and feels alone in a world that isn't providing her diddlysquat at this moment.

"How about I let you say the F-word twenty times in a row right now, will that help?"

To my delight, Nina smiles. "Look how beautiful you are when you smile," I say.

"I'm not smiling for you." She quickly sets me straight.

Nina contracts for safety, meaning she agrees not to harm herself—at least not tonight. She signs a piece of paper with a date on, and I finally get her settled in bed.

"I'll be back to check on you momentarily," I tell her.

To be honest, I have a bit of a soft spot for Nina. She reminds me of my younger self in that I hated my mother with a passion for a long,

long time. The hatred I carried made me angry and hard. I felt the world owed me and I certainly owed it nothing in return. "Fuck all y'all," I believe was the exact sentiment attached to my teen-hood. I understand the feisty fury that bubbles through Nina, and, in a way, I admire her for it. I mean, at this point, Nina has bitten her mother on the arm and shot her mother in the face. Why didn't I think of doing that to my mother? I'm impressed by Nina's insolence and audacity. She's a pill, and she's making damn sure that people (mainly her mother) choke when they try to swallow her. Go Nina. Fight Nina. Don't give up. Don't give in — 'cos you're fighting for your preservation. You are championing yourself. Do it.

I'd like to tell Nina how I admire her hutzpah, but I doubt that the shelter director would condone me paying Nina respect for her full-blown teenage rebellion.

Within a few minutes, I sneak back upstairs to check on the girls, hoping they'll be asleep. No such luck. They're awake, and I can hear them whispering.

"I can't believe you tried to kill your dad." Nina low whistles in amazement.

"Yeah, me either." Shondah murmurs. "Thank God he was okay."

They fall silent, and I'm about to enter when Shondah whispers loudly: "You shot your mother in the face."

More silence. Then both girls burst out laughing. I can't help chuckling myself and decide not to interrupt. They're bonding and that will help them both. Sometimes it is what the residents get from each other and the peer-bonds they form that help them the most. It's the relief of finding someone in the same predicament; someone who has similar concerns and fears as oneself. This eases the sense of "I am all alone" and "no one understands what I'm going through."

Hopefully, Nina will fare better this time around at the shelter. I want that for her.

Hopefully, I will fare better this time around with Roy as well. I want that for me.

CHAPTER 19

Captain, oh my Captain

My flight to Wyoming leaves at 10:30 a.m. and amazingly, I'm not nervous about this upcoming flight. It appears that if Roy factors into the equation, I *can* be sealed into a steel sarcophagus — willingly and joyfully (and of course, with 10 mg of Xanax because pharmaceuticals aren't always bad).

I arrive at the airport in ample time and join a dismally long line. Everyone is traveling for New Year's Eve. Time ticks away as I wait patiently, no need to stress. Everything is going to be fine. Roy misses me and wants me back. Billowing with elation, I don't notice how quickly the time passes. When I finally get to the counter, the United Airlines woman eyes me.

"The gate for your flight is already closed," she says. "You should've arrived earlier. I'm sorry but you've missed your flight."

What? I mean...WHAT? Excuse me crazy ticket counter lady but if you don't let me on the plane, I'm going to explode right here, right now — a terminal incident in an incidental terminal.

"But I *was* here on time." I fume. "I've been standing in this stupid line for almost an hour. Why didn't you guys call me? Why not make an announcement for those with flights leaving soon to step ahead in line? What kind of a nonsensical set up is this?" My frantic need to get on that plane is making me rather aggressive.

"You need to calm down, ma'am," the suddenly smug counter lady says.

Oh no, you didn't. You didn't just tell me to calm down. My blood pressure spikes. A vein threatens to rupture in my left temple.

"Do you realize that when people are experiencing stress, asking them to calm down only escalates them?" I snap at her. "Did you know that?" By now my voice has a thin, tin quality to it. I am escalating. My reasoning powers are succumbing to "lizard brain".

"I can place you on standby for the next flight" she says, a slight smile on her face.

What the fuck? Is she enjoying this?

"Standby? Does that mean I'm not even guaranteed a seat on the next plane?"

"It's New Year's Eve ma'am, the flights are pretty full."

I hate this woman with such intensity. It makes me sweaty.

"So, let me get on my flight." I plead. "The plane hasn't left yet."

I'm about to unleash further hostility on her, when two security guards flank me. I have to tilt my head up to read a badge attached to a large chest bulging in my face: Head of Security. This head honcho is huge. I start jabbering to his chest.

"I need to get on my flight. It hasn't left yet, and they won't give me a boarding pass. I have to get to Wyoming." Tears prick my eyes. No, no. I don't want to cry now. No one respects tears. "I have to get to Wyoming." I repeat stubbornly.

"You need to come with us, ma'am." Head honcho says as he takes a hold of my arm to steer me away from the counter.

"There's no need to touch me," I yap at him and tug my arm away. Of course, I am doing all the wrong things—but then, so is he. And I'm the one that is having a meltdown, not him. He should take the high road here and understand...yeah right. He's an airport security guard, not a therapist. He squeezes my arm tighter and marches me away from the crowd.

"You still need to go through security check, ma'am; therefore you won't make your plane on time."

He leaves me at the security check, where I am meticulously searched. Airport security rummage through items from my hand luggage. They frisk me. They swab my shoes. Apparently, they're looking for chemical residue from any bomb-making spree I may have been on. It's not like I have a classic "unabomber" look, and I'd certainly prefer to be thought of as a bombshell, not a bomb-maker.

Once they're done searching me, I'm escorted to the allocated gate to wait for my "standby" flight. On reaching the gate, I realize that right across the way they are still boarding my original plane. I march up to the counter and confront the lady working there.

"I want to get on this plane." I demand. "I bought a ticket for this plane, and they said I wouldn't be here in time, but look, here I am, and I want to get on *this* plane."

"I'm sorry ma'am," the United woman tells me. "You are now scheduled for the next flight and your luggage has been sent to that holding bay."

Arrrgghh! My frustration level is peaking. I'm pretty keen to lean over the counter and yank on the nice lady's hair, or at least slap the counter top. What the hell is wrong with this airline? They're messing with my special New Year's Eve reunification with my beloved. Do they have any idea how important that is? Do they? Do they?

As I stand before the United woman, my muscles twitching with indignation, a large shadow steps into my peripheral vision. Too preoccupied with forming a stinging torrent of primo insults to hurl about, I pay little attention to the newcomer.

"If this young lady doesn't get on the plane," the large shadow announces, "then neither do I."

Uh...Hello? What's that?

"And you'll need me," the man continues "because I'm the captain."

Jaw muscles fail me completely. My mouth flops open as I stare idiotically at my knight in shining uniform. He winks at me. This priceless pilot instructs the annoying woman to fetch my suitcase from the other holding bay (in the rain, no less), and I am most excellently vindicated. Showing decorum, I refrain from flashing a self-satisfied smirk her way, and board my flight with close to euphoria in my heart. Yay, yay, yay! I'm going to get to see Roy on New Year's Eve after all. Excitement overload—that's yippy times a million.

He is there to greet me at the airport. My heart does summersaults the minute I see him. That face. That smile. I frickin love this guy. I love him so much it makes me feel genuinely sick.

We hop in his car and head towards his uncle's ranch. I prattle away, telling him how I almost missed the flight, how this lovely captain saved the day for me, how the nasty woman had to retrieve my bag in the rain. I omit the part where I hugged the captain at the end of the flight and told him that I loved him forever. Nor do I share that the captain was damn good looking. I'm not stupid. I know that Roy might distort my story, until suddenly, because I hugged the captain, I am a slut from the backwaters of Slutville.

We arrive at his uncle's house and hit the booze immediately. By midnight we've danced and smoked and laughed and danced some more (not very well, I might add—but hey, drunk dancing is awesome), and I'm convinced that our relationship is back on terra firma once more. Praise be to Jesus, Buddha and all other deities too.

We bring in the New Year with a lengthy and rather energetic sex session, which is highly unusual for Roy, not so much for me, because I quite possibly am a slut from the backwaters of Slutville. It's remarkable what champagne, wine and Jägermeister can do to your libido…and your flexibility. While flinging each other about the bed, giggling and shushing one another, groping and gripping in the dark, I realize that this is the most relaxed Roy has ever been in this department. Look at us in flagrante delicto, and Roy, finally being playful. I love him when he's playful. Oh please, who am I kidding? I love him even when he's as serious as a Puritan Priest, which he usually is in the sex department—thank you, silly, verkrampfed religious upbringing.

And what about my upbringing? Well, I do note that I'm hanging on to an image of the captain while having sex with Roy for as long as possible, because subconsciously I know that Roy's going to dump me again. On some level it's nice to know that I can actually feel attracted to someone else. Maybe there can be a life without Roy after all? Sure, as long as it is filled with another man. Heaven forbid that I be by myself and work on my own shit. Yeah, who does that?

Our time in Wyoming is lighthearted fun. We skid about on a frozen lake, we build a snowman, we beam each other with snowballs, we play scrabble with Roy's uncle, and he annihilates us every time (I attribute his scrabble skills to the sheer monotony of housebound captivity during the months of subzero temperatures). I trust that Roy and I are an item once again. Oh, happy, happy day.

Our drive back to California is a five-day journey, where each successive day is more wonderful than the last. We are so comfortable together. We fit. Now, don't be surprised, but we stay at casinos every night (you didn't see that one coming, did you?) We party like champions and I even try my hand at gambling. I choose Black Jack, and since it's my first time sitting at a table, I have no idea what I'm doing. I instantly break the rules. I touch my neighbor's cards, I touch the croupier in an attempt to high five him, and I lift both my hands off the table (something like that). In a flash, the pit boss strides over and asks me to vamoose. 'Tis probably a good thing because I've had buckets to drink and I'm flooded with generosity and daring—you wanna bet $2000?

    I stagger up to our hotel room and flop down on the bed. At some point, Roy comes in and takes ahold of my hand. I can't help myself. I start to cry. The horrible drunk grief thing where you can't stop, and you become a hiccupping, mucus vending machine—highly unattractive.

    "I know you don't love me," I slur out, "'cos I sing in bars and I'm not virtuous and I can't make cinnamon buns or chicken casseroles."

    Roy actually looks crestfallen. He writes on a napkin and leaves it by the bedside, so I can read it in the morning when I'm sober: "I don't want you to ever feel ashamed for who you are. I like who you are!"

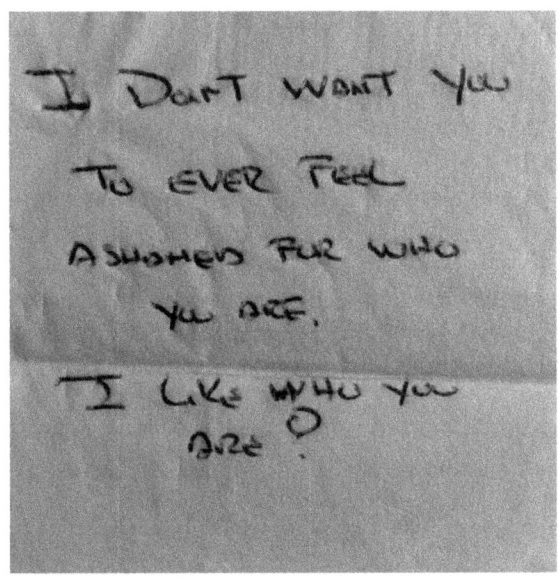

I keep the napkin (for years), but what Roy has written doesn't really help me, since he's the one who is telling me I'm not virtuous, nor quality marriage material, and that my abilities in the kitchen are pitiful. Maybe he does like who I am, but he doesn't *love* who I am, nor does he want to spend the rest of his life with who I am. As I inherently suspected, on the final day, when we are less than 50 miles from home, Roy pulls the plug.

"Just because we did this trip together," he declares, "don't think that we are back on as a couple."

I stare out the car window at ginormous clouds that up until a split second ago had seemed incredibly beautiful. My heart pitches up into my throat. I don't look at Roy. I focus on the clouds.

"Plus, I realize that I can't see you at all anymore. It's just hurting you, so...no more." His eyes stay on the road as he speaks—he won't even look at me.

Clouds, Niki. Focus. Don't cry. Look at the clouds. They look as beautiful whether you are part of a couple or not. The world is still an amazing adventure to be had, whether you experience it with Roy, or experience it alone. Well, shit, no. That's not quite true. The clouds suddenly mock me from above, retracting all their beauty, as if beauty is a thing reserved solely for those in love. Everything turns bleak and dire without Roy. My whole world starts sliding into grey. And not fifty shades of grey, which might be better—no, solomente uno shade—dark grey gloom.

Fuck.

So, you know what I do when I get home? Yes, you are correct. I write a letter to the captain. I tell him how wonderful he is and how I'd like to take him for a drink to say thank you (which translated means: I'm desperate, please captain, how about *you* marry me?) However, the United Airlines website doesn't operate quite the same way as Tinder, and therefore the captain never receives my gushing missive.

CHAPTER 20

The Mourning

It's really sinking in. The fact that I can never again sleep alongside my beloved, hold his hand, touch his face, see his crinkly smile, or hear the voice that pleases my very innermost ears. The reality is too overwhelming for me and my whole body revolts against it. I can no longer sleep, or eat, or sit still, or think rational thoughts. My shoulders sag forward and my back hunches over as if suddenly it's too much effort to hold myself upright. My spine is disintegrating, collapsing me into the shape of a question mark. It's my physical being shouting out: Why? Why? Why? Why doesn't he love me anymore?

Full-blown terror wells up and engulfs me.

"Samantha, I'm selling the house," I inform my child. "We're moving."

It takes me all of 5 minutes to make this momentous decision, to sell the home where Samantha and I have lived for the past nine years. Inexplicably, I hate our mobile home with a blazing passion. I hate the filthy mobile home park too, and all the repulsive people that live in it. Maybe Roy would have loved me more if I didn't live in such a shit hole.

I hate my life. Hate it. I've messed up everything. EVERYTHING. My whole life has been one massive mistake. I've made one poor choice after another. Roy is right. Singing in bars is glum, working for peanuts at the shelter is dismal, living in a mobile home is depressing, being illegal is shit, being a single mother is depressing. What the fuck? Have I simply had my head shoved really far up my own ass?

How have I not noticed how appalling my life is until now? I hate myself. I don't want to be me any longer. I can't bear it. Help me, I'm freaking out.
Can't stay in my skin for one more minute
I'm going fucking crazy in it.

Thus, my knee jerk reaction to sell the house—here is something I *can* rectify. I slap a "For Sale" sign in our living room window and within four days I receive an offer for my place. I don't counter offer. I don't haggle. I don't care. I take it. $45k. That's forty-five thousand dollars. More money than I've ever had in my life. Still, that brings me hardly any comfort. I pack everything up and before you can say "deep vein thrombosis" (which is rather fun to say), Samantha and I have moved in with the Moore family.

Please allow me to take a moment to say, thank you Moore family for generously allowing us to infiltrate your living space—I very much appreciate it.

Samantha stays in Brooke's room with Brookie, and I stay in Brett's room without Brett. Brett is Brooke's older brother, who is away at college, but his room still looks like a six-year-old lives there. It's the dinosaur wallpaper and little planes hanging from the ceiling that make it so.

Two weeks into my mourning, I'm offered a part time job at a music studio as an audio engineer. In case you were wondering, I have been an audio engineer before—and in fact, I was quite good at it. Grateful for any distraction, I accept the position and soon sit with a notepad scribbling down information about the outboard gear, the various programs, and how things operate at this particular studio. Although I've done this gig before, I cannot for the life of me, figure out this new studio. Nothing I scribble down makes sense. My brain is pretty much out of commission. The guy who is training me must think I'm an idiot. I keep asking him to repeat things and need to excuse myself every so often to go and cry in the bathroom. I'm simply unable to function. It's not long before they call me into the office and sit me down for the bad news. I know I'm being fired, and before they can even start speaking, my heart thumps so erratically that I tell my soon to be ex-boss "I think I might need to go to hospital."

Who knew grieving could be so all encompassing. So painful. So exhausting. I cry in the shower. I cry in my car. I cry in public restrooms. I cry in unexpected places at inopportune times. I even cry in my sleep for crying in a bucket (which is a curious saying, although, no doubt, I could fill a bucket by merely conjuring Roy's face). It's chronically depressing and completely draining. I've become a blubbering mess with the energy level of a dead slug and now have the self-esteem of a vomit bag. How did this happen? I used to be fearless and svelte, self-assured and irrepressible? How did I become this dismal heap? I've been crushed, that's what happened. My outlook on life has swung from "oh glorious day" to "oh endless fucking day."

How on earth am I going to get through this?

My whole world is falling apart. The mistake I've made, that I am as yet unable to see, is that I've placed everything on Roy. Roy was supposed to save me, marry me, support me, introduce me to Hollywood, jolt my music career to life, move me into a mansion, swoop me to the land of milk and honey, and basically make my life outstandingly tremendous. I systematically built a whole fantasy life for myself based on Roy's being. And now that Roy's being no longer wishes to "be" in my fantasy picture, I am flat-out terrified. I'm begging and fighting and struggling, and willing to do anything to keep my beautiful world from collapsing back into the old dreary world of poverty, loneliness, and illegality. My view of myself changes drastically, too. With a partner, I was hot, sexy, clever, funny, desirable, cute and lithe. Without a partner, I'm suddenly old, haggard, pathetic, clumsy, vaguely disgusting, and desperately in need of a drink.

The drink part I can fix. Hence, I haul my old haggard, pathetic, clumsy, vaguely disgusting self off to try my usual ruse of drinking the ghastliness away. I decide to go to the Harp Inn (a short drive from the Moore house) and plan to drink myself into oblivion. Perhaps I can drink myself off the face of this earth? I'll sure give it a damn good try. And yes, I drive to the Harp Inn with the full intention of getting blitzed and then driving back home—it's only 3 blocks, is what I tell myself.

Slamming back drink after drink, I morph into a lively, animated, drop-dead sex-bomb (granted this is only in my mind as no one is dropping dead in my presence—slumping over maybe). As men gather around me, I loudly inform them that I will marry anyone who can A) spell diarrhea (because you know that's my party trick) and B) supply me with a washer/dryer. I don't think this is too much to ask for. Woefully, no one can spell diarrhea, and eventually, neither can I.

It's at this point that some random guy proposes I go home with him.

"Let's take your car," he suggests.

"Sure." I slur out. I'm easy prey at this moment. I'd happily go home with Jack the Ripper and drunkenly presume he must own a Maytag, or a Whirlpool, and most likely excelled in spelling bees.

Random guy drives me to his apartment and soon we're horizontal on his double bed. He's all hot to trot, and me? I burst into tears, my cheerful drunk dissolving into an unstoppable, crushing misery. I can't lie next to him. What would Roy say? I stagger over to a couch and flop down to howl. I sob uncontrollably for at least an hour. I simply can't stop. Snot pours out of me, gunking up Random's couch. I'm seriously fouling up his bachelor haven.

At first Random tries to comfort me, cajole me back into his bed, coax me to stop crying. Eventually he's begging me to leave.

"Go the fuck home, lady!" he screams at me.

Sorry dude, but I'm temporarily out of order—ruptured down the middle like a spatchcocked chicken. I'm useless. Sob, sob, sob, is my only answer. Besides, I can't "go the fuck home" because I've sold my house and now live in a bedroom where dinosaurs and small planes romp the walls, while my daughter is crammed into a bedroom downstairs with Brookie.

Random eventually passes out. He snores softly while I continue hiccupping and gulping and basically coming unglued on his settee.

It's a lengthy lamentation, but finally, I cry myself out and manage to pull it together enough to leave. I fumble my way out of Random's apartment only to wander wretchedly about trying to locate my car. Random lives in one of those soul-sucking apartment complexes where everything looks the same. The ugly urban uniformity of some bastard architect who must really fancy the color of my favorite spelling word—diarrhea (of the mud-brown variety).

This suburban prison has a layered car park and I have no idea which level my car is on. On the third level, my car waits patiently for me, and I'm so relieved to climb into it and drive off. It's 4 a.m. and I'm exhausted.

On exiting the car park, I stare stupidly at a bright green cone in the middle of the road that blocks my way. In my still drunk state, the green cone appeals to me, and I have no idea why, but for some reason, I *must* have it. I drive up alongside the cone, open my car door, lean out; basically hanging out of my car and grab it. I fling the green treasure behind me onto my back seat and as I straighten up, I now notice the three police cars on the opposite side of the road.

Oh, fuck me. I'm in mega shit now.

Even though there are approximately eight officers standing right in front of me and I've just stolen one of their road markings, for some inexplicable reason, they don't notice me. How implausibly lucky is that? I quietly drive away, willing my car to slink by and keep its hood down.

Back in my dinosaur refuge, I wake to the sound of the jacuzzi kicking on. It comes on automatically at 9 a.m. every morning and it quickly becomes my therapy pool. I establish a routine for the mornings of my mourning. I sink into warm bubbles and allow my arms to float up. I become weightless and thoughtless. I sit completely still and listen to the birds and the bubbles, and try to calm my mind.

There's a thermometer bobbing in the tub and I think to myself "if that thermometer comes over and touches me, then that will mean that Roy is coming back to me". The little temperature gauge obliges and drifts over to nestle against my back. Oh, fortunate fortune! Roy will be returning. The universe is sending me a clear sign. Well, perhaps not *that* clear, because the bobbing fortuneteller drifts away and is soon back, drifts away and hits me again and again as it rotates in the jacuzzi. I'm nothing more than a pitiful, pudgy, hungover obstacle in its path.

I'm going a little crazy—I have an unattractive meltdown in Arloa's kitchen one day. Thankfully, none of the Moore family are home to witness this, only Samantha. I'm trying to cook (not my strongest talent as I've mentioned) and Samantha innocently asks what the hell *am* I making? And why does it smell so revolting? Well, I'm making cabbage and it is pungent, but Samantha commenting on an odor shouldn't bring the world to an end. Nonetheless, this small amount of criticism is the straw that breaks my momentarily feeble back. I lose my shit completely. I hurl cabbage about the kitchen, making a huge mess. Some part of me finds extraordinary release in flinging a member of the cruciferous family about the kitchen, while another part of me is appalled at the childish behavior I'm exhibiting in front of my daughter. Yet I can't stop myself. It's a vaguely out-of-body like experience. For Samantha, it seems to be a confirmation that her mother is ridiculous because... "You're ridiculous," she says. "Totally ridiculous."

Goddammit! I know. I know. I know.

I gulp for air as my hands start to tingle. Shit, that's a panic attack coming for sure. I engage an alternate nostril breathing technique that I know will help slow my breathing down. I've taught this very trick to numerous kids at the shelter—oh, if they could only see me now.

It's not easy to calm yourself down once your bloodstream is raging with adrenaline, so I silently congratulate myself on being cognizant enough to engage this Buddha-breathing practice. Plug one nostril and breathe in through the open airway, then swap fingers, and breathe out through the opposite nostril.

"It looks like your snorting cocaine," Samantha scoffs mercilessly.

"I'm sick of you judging me." I scream at her. Yup, I'm practically a Tibetan monk.

"You're embarrassing yourself," Samantha enlightens me further and leaves, unwilling to engage with me any further.

Yes, I am. I *am* embarrassing myself, and once I compose myself (by pretending to snort cocaine, I might add), I feel thoroughly ashamed.

Samantha and I can't find common ground. Our relationship is strained. I want Samantha to be supportive and understand that I'm suffering an enormous heartache, but she thinks I'm childish and silly, and that Roy is not worth shedding one tear over. She's actually right. Roy is not worth all this emotional havoc, and in truth, it isn't solely Roy that is causing my pain—he has merely triggered it. His rejection of me has brought deep-seated issues to the surface. This crushing grief I'm feeling is a breakdown of everything—my entire life up until this point. I'm heartbroken that my music career has never amounted to anything. I tried so hard, for so long, and held such hope. I'm heartbroken that I'm seemingly incapable of having a relationship that lasts longer than 10 months. What is wrong with me? Mainly, I'm heartbroken that my mother was never there for me and that I've always felt abandoned. Yes, I'm 38 and still pine for a mother—does that ever go away? Just to clear things up, my mother was physically there, it's just that her noodles had slipped off her plate and mothering was not something she was capable of doing.

So, this break up has ruptured me wide open. Now I must find a way to piece myself back together. Roy leaving is really just the tip of the iceberg.

"He's an asshole." Samantha reminds me.

We're in a parking lot, sitting in my car, and I choose this moment to confront Samantha.

"Look, I know you're a teenager, and teens are supposed to hate their parents. I get it. I really do."

And the thing is, since I work with teens all day long, I really do get it.

"It's healthy for you to break away from me." I continue. "You're individuating; becoming your own person. I'm all for that. It's basically your job to hate me right now. "

Samantha nods adamantly in full agreement.

"All I'm asking is that you maybe stop doing your job so well." I smile at her. "I'm sorry I'm useless right now, but I will recover, and meanwhile, can you go easy on me? Once I'm back on my feet you can unleash as much hatred on me as you need."

"I don't hate you, mom," Samantha says thoughtfully. "I love you, but you're annoying as hell."

All I hear is "I love you" and have to fight the urge to weep. Thank you, God. This precious human loves me, and that makes everything okay. Almost.

CHAPTER 21

Unfair Trade

It's hard to work at the shelter and be heart broken. How can I present a happy face for the residents, or encourage and support them, when I'm dead inside? How can I listen to their problems when all I want to do is blurt out: "oh, you think *your* life is shit?"

The fact that I'm heftily hungover doesn't help either…don't try this at home kids. How crazy that when I tell people I work at a shelter they give me major kudos and frequently tell me that I'm a saint. Yes sure, Saint Gin of Tonic maybe.

Today I'm "babysitting" our newest resident, an autistic boy named John. John is fairly high functioning (certainly better functioning than I am at the moment), but he feels threatened easily. Everything seems suspicious to him. Since I feel as unprotected as a snail without a shell, I can relate to John's vulnerability. I'm careful around him and take the time to explain things clearly to him so he doesn't jump to conclusions. For example, John notices a group of volunteers working in the yard. The volunteers are here to take down the Christmas lights, but John's convinced that they are here solely to make fun of him. A friendly, well-meaning volunteer comes to the front door and introduces himself.

"Hi, I'm Lyle."

"Zip it, buddy!" John snarls, and slams the door in his face.

The good thing about working at the shelter while having a broken heart is that it serves as a distraction, and since I'm experiencing my day in a peculiar disconnected way, being at the shelter is almost like watching a TV show. I watch as John sneezes a wad of green stuff onto his own shirt and then freaks out.

"I'm sick, I'm deathly ill," he laments loudly. "This shelter is riddled with disease. It's making me sick."

John swipes at the green stuff with a tissue. "Bring me my penguin book, hurry!" he shouts. "You know I'm going to live in Honolulu."

John's all-over-the-show thought process is another thing I can relate to at the moment. My thoughts are similar: "I'm old—deathly old. I'm going to die alone. I'm rotting away in this shelter job. Bring me vodka, hurry! You know, I'm going to live in a dinosaur den for the rest of my life".

John asks if I'd like to help him do a jigsaw puzzle, and soon we sit side by side piecing together a complicated Rembrandt painting. In the background, ethereal music plays—John has chosen an Enya CD that momentarily lulls me. As the puzzle takes shape a surge of gratitude hits me and I find myself silently thanking John for babysitting me.

Another positive thing about being at the shelter during my heartache is that the children I work with are genuinely suffering, and this helps shift my perspective on my own pain—at least for a few hours.

One such shift in perspective is Graham, a cute 13-year-old who was adopted at age seven. His adoptive parents, both lawyers, understood how to work the adoption process in their favor. It can be very problematic to adopt, and can take months, but these lawyers adopted Graham in record time without a hitch.

Graham behaved well for the first few years with his new family, but as puberty hit him, he started questioning if outgrowing his cute little boy phase would lessen his parent's love for him? As his body transformed into the voice-cracking, hair-sprouting, pimple-spreading, hormone-raging, gruesomeness that is teen-hood, Graham's insecurities kicked into high gear. He started to act up.

Lots of adopted kids struggle with deep-seated insecurity, and who can blame them? After all, their core caregivers, their life-blood, did reject them. And this "core rejection" sometimes brings up the need to test their new parents in an effort to determine if they can be trusted.

How far can they push these new parents before they, too, abandon ship?

With his teen angst stacked on top of his underlying self-doubt, Graham has been repeatedly testing his parents in a 'will-they-still-love-me-if-I-do-this' setup.

Part of my training as shelter staff includes a series of workshops on adoption. These workshops cover what parents should know before getting into an adoption situation; what they should prepare for, and what they can expect. I remember a sad example of a little five-year-old boy who kept pooping in the doorway of his parent's bedroom. It drove them crazy, but every time the young boy felt insecure, he would plop one in their doorframe. In his young mind, he figured, "if they can forgive me for this, then that means they love me, right?"

Graham has been "testing" his parents for the past year and his tests have grown increasingly reckless. To date, he has smashed their patio windows, stolen money from them, and snuck into the neighbor's house to order porno on their cable TV. His parents are pretty much done being understanding. The final straw comes when Graham keys their brand-new BMW. The lawyer parents fail "the Graham test" miserably. Graham freely admits that he scratched their BMW and tells his parents it's because he thinks they love the car more than they love him. He confesses that he felt envious and was unable to control the impulse to lash out at them. They respond by bringing Graham to the shelter. They hope that the shelter can help "straighten" him out.

The problem is that Graham is right; his parents do care more about their car than him—and their house, and their lifestyle, and how they appear to the neighbors. Graham is right to worry, because his parents *did* think he was great when he was a cute, seven-year-old that the neighbors could coo over. They're not as enamored of him now that he is a gangling, awkward, scowling teenager with anger issues.

It's no wonder that Graham's angry and scowling most of the time. He hasn't had much therapy and hasn't yet worked through his fundamental abandonment issues. As stated earlier, when you've been rejected by the person who brings you into this world it can make you wonder, "What the hell is wrong with me? Why couldn't my biological parents love me?"

In trying to cope with his ongoing anxiety, Graham has taken to lying, cheating, and stealing, all in a futile attempt to bolster himself. Sadly, his parents don't recognize his defiance as a cry for acceptance and love. Instead they are punitive and cold, and poor Graham keeps inadvertently pushing the very affection he craves further and further away from himself. At this point, Graham's parents are fed up. They choose not take Graham on family weekend outings (which are optional), claiming they need a break from their son. Following several heated family sessions (which are not optional), they decide they need a permanent break.

"We wish to relinquish our rights to Graham," they tell their therapist.

The therapist shares this update with us during staff meeting, and I'm incensed on Graham's behalf.

"Can they do that?" I ask.

Apparently yes, they can, and since they're both lawyers, they know this. I sit in the meeting, fuming. My inside voice rants: "You can't give back a child. It's crushing for Graham. How will he recuperate from that low blow? Who will ever be able to convince him that they *do* want to be with him? He already has attachment issues up the wazoo. His relationships are going to be so fucked up. He's going to need sooo much therapy, and good therapists are few and far between....and why the fuck *did* Roy leave me? What's wrong with me? Am *I* unlovable?" And so on, and so on.

Graham takes the news fairly calmly. He asks where he will live next and which school he will attend. He would like to stay at his same school, but that seems unlikely. I grow very fond of Graham and discover he wants to learn to play guitar. Excellent—here is something I *can* do for him. I draw him chord charts and teach him finger positions, coaching him until he can play a few songs. Graham's birthday is coming up, and since I've a gig playing at the Orange

County Fair on that same day, I ask the shelter director to agree to allow the kids to come to my show.

    The OC Fair is a big gig (see? My pop star life is not completely dead—it still twitches once in a while). I'm thrilled that the shelter kids are in attendance and am eager to acknowledge them. Of course, I don't say: "the kids from the shelter are here"—I say: "I'd like to thank my young friends for coming out." Their little faces shine as the audience applauds for them.

    After I've played a few songs, I call Graham up on stage and ask the crowd to help me sing him happy birthday. He stands grinning from ear to ear. He's adorable… and so excited…and it pleases me deeply to be able to give him this experience.

    I only wish I could do more for him. I toy with the idea of adopting him. I wish I could adopt him, but I have no money. Only this low paying job, and a young daughter that I can hardly manage, and well, there's a myriad of reasons why I can't help Graham more—the main one being, I can hardly help myself. I might be a good performer on stage, but my performance in real life is not quite as remarkable.

Late one afternoon the following week, Graham's parents come by the shelter to drop off his belongings. Although Graham is desperate to see them, they've made it clear that they will not oblige him with a visit. The therapist has warned staff that Graham's parents are coming by, and we're told to distract him, to keep him busy and away from the front door. We don't want him to know that his parents (or ex-parents) are within reach. I notice their fancy BMW pull up and hasten to make sure that Graham is occupied playing basketball with staff in the backyard. There's no doubt it's his parents arriving because their BMW has a deep, violent scratch down the right side.

    Round about now, I'm thinking that the scratch may not be totally undeserved. In fact, at this point, I'm keen to go out there and scratch their car myself; maybe even their faces. I'll most certainly stare some hatful looks at them as soon as they step inside. But neither parent comes inside. The woman stays in the car, while the man hurriedly drops Graham's belongings off on the doorstep. He rings the bell and hustles back to his fancy car as quickly as possible. It's a dirty deed he's doing, and I bet that on some level, he 100% knows it.

As I stare daggers at their car, I notice a young boy in the back seat. A boy of about seven years old. Who is that, I wonder? Graham doesn't have any siblings, and this couple doesn't strike me as the kind who would offer to babysit. They drive away with the little kid in the back seat and I can't bear it. I let staff know the coast is clear and because I now require some counseling myself, I go hunt down the therapist.

"They had a kid in the car with them," I raise an eyebrow at her.

"The nerve of those people," the therapist shakes her head in disbelief. "Unbelievable."

"Did they adopt another ..."

She cuts me off. "They sure did. I can't believe they had the gall to bring him along in the car. Don't let Graham know."

Of course, I won't let Graham know, but how can these "parents" do that? How is that legal? They're lawyers, I guess they must have figured it out.

"But you can't trade in children. Surely it doesn't work like that. Can't we report them?" I want these lawyer charlatans stopped.

"To whom?" The therapist looks at me.

"To anyone who will listen."

"Don't let him find out, it will break his heart." She shoos me out of her office.

I have to take a moment. I hide in the bathroom and cry. Why is there such an enormous lack of love on this earth? I'm broken hearted for Graham and floored by the unfairness of it all. You can't trade your biological children in, how come you are allowed to do so with adopted kids? And quickly my thoughts careen back to Roy. Is that Roy's plan? Is that why he broke up with me? So he could swap me out for a newer, younger version? Oh, foul thought.

Suddenly it seems that love is all that matters—in the world, in the universe, in infinity and beyond. A rush of dread hits me hard. I *must* have love. I must. Someone must love me right now or I will die. Like I said, the kid's anguish only shifts my perspective for a short time.

CHAPTER 22

Sandbag Me

It's during my vulnerable mourning period that the shelter's director, Colleen, decides to accept another position within the organization and transfers to head office. Colleen has been at the shelter as long as I have, and I'm bummed that she's moving on. I should be moving on. I'm stuck in my low-paid job and have been for 12 years. God, I'm a failure, and my prospects are zero unless my pop star dream suddenly decides to transpire...yeah right. No wonder Roy dumped me.

Colleen's replacement, a feisty woman from New York, brings with her a whole different approach on how the shelter should be run. During our usual Tuesday staff infection, we welcome Trudy to her new position.

Dressed in a knee-length skirt that hikes up as she sits down, Trudy reclines with her legs open, allowing staff to glimpse her dark places. What's going on here, Sharon Stone?

"So, how do we deal with these little fuckers?" she asks in a loud, demanding, nasally New York accent.

There is a stunned silence. No one says anything. How can we? We're gob smacked. Surely she isn't referring to our clients as "little fuckers"? And surely she is aware that we can see up her skirt?

"In New York, we call a spade a spade," she starts in on us. "We don't pussyfoot around like you Californians do. You people here don't have the balls to speak your mind, and that makes for an uncomfortable work environment."

Is she insulting us now?

"If you have a problem with one of your work mates, tell them. Don't come to me with your petty grievances. You guys sort it out between yourselves. Get over your namby-pamby 'got to be the nice guy' crap."

Oh yeah? Well, it's impossible for us to sort out our problems with each other while working on the floor. Firstly, we have to perform as a cohesive unit in front of the "little fuckers" or they'll smell weakness and manipulate us round the clock. Secondly, the staff at the shelter are composed of people of a certain ilk. We're drawn to this work exactly because we are softies, and being softies, we do not like confrontations. Our altruism has us being kind to our fellow workers, even when they are fucking up quite royally. And thirdly, the staff fucks up quite royally fairly often, and then to confuse matters, they are sometimes rewarded for their fuck ups. At this point, we're at a bit of a loss as to what is, and what isn't, correct behavior for staff.

Please allow me to give you an example: A large percentage of our clients are placed on a one-on-one (1:1) watch. In other words, one staff member must be with said client at all times. If the client needs to use the bathroom, a staff member must wait outside the door. It's pretty clear-cut stuff, yet twice we've had kids run away while they were on a 1:1 watch. One time, the kid absconded through their bedroom window while their assigned staff member was playing games with the other residents in the living room. And here's the corker—on that occasion the staff was commended on how well they handled the situation. Flummoxing, right? Does a 1:1 mean if there is a game being enjoyed, like say Monopoly, then staff should not worry too much about the client that's on a round-the-clock guard, and permit said client to go unsupervised to their bedroom? Then not bother to check on them for the next few hours, as long as they follow protocol and call the police once the kid has bolted from the shelter? I guess so.

We even had a resident run from the shelter while wearing an ankle bracelet that monitored her movements. She ran to the nearest grocery store where she stole a pair of scissors and proceeded to hack through her ankle monitor. The monitor proved trickier than she'd anticipated, and she ended up hacking into her ankle by mistake. Hobbling back to the shelter, bleeding and freaked out, she told staff what had happened. No one had even noticed she was gone—and so much for the ankle monitor.

"Californians talk shit behind your back," our new boss continues. "In New York, we'll say that shit right to your face."
Turns out on this one, Trudy is 100 % correct. One by one, staff find their way to head office to "talk shit" about the new director behind her rather broad and arrogant New York back. Trudy is on some bizarre ego power trip and is utterly inappropriate for the shelter, consequently, there are soon enough complaints against her and she is fired. Phew!

Not phew for long though, because Trudy is quickly replaced by Lisa, who, God help us, is even worse. Unfortunately, to compound matters, the headcheese has handpicked our new 'new' director from another program within the agency, where apparently, she's done excellent work. Lisa has won herself the position of teacher's pet. Drat. The headcheese loves Lisa. Shit, shit, shit.
Lisa is on the opposite end of the spectrum from Trudy. Lisa speaks in a wispy voice and wants to treat the teens with "kids gloves" as if they were five-year-old children. Her previous position saw her surrounded by young children, so it's not hard to understand where she's coming from, but here at the shelter, we are dealing with teenagers; sometimes pretty hardcore ones at that.
When Lisa recommends that we learn "love and logic", a treatment plan that includes recommendations like: "we give treats to those that brush their teeth," I'm tempted to flatten her with a sarcastic mocking of: "well, here we give treats to those that don't stab their parents."
We're not dealing with five-year-olds, and our teens not brushing their teeth is certainly on the low end of the problem scale round here. As Lisa continues in her soft baby voice, it comes to my attention that not only does she have one set voice level, she further has one set facial expression. It's hard to read her. Is she happy? Is she upset?

Annoyed maybe? There's something distinctly disturbing about her placid face. Being pale and a little on the heavy side, I can't help it but soon I find myself thinking of her as an expressionless sandbag.

    The expressionless sandbag must sense my contempt for her "love and logic" and her soft baby voice, because she takes an instantaneous dislike to me. She sends me an email giving me extra graveyard duties. She wants me to cut out pictures from magazines and sort the pictures into different folders labeled: cars, houses, travel, animals etc. I'm further instructed to cut out words and place those in a separate folder. This is so our clients can make poster board collages of images and words to describe themselves in their "This is Me" projects. Okay, that's great—and we've been doing that for years at the shelter, except the kids have always cut out their own pictures and chosen their own words.

    I politely write back.

Hi Lisa

I believe that the residents choosing their own pictures, cutting their own shapes and using their own words is therapeutic for them—same as you expressed in your email saying knitting and crocheting are therapeutic—I believe the act of actually cutting and perusing the magazines has a similar calming effect. Us spoon feeding pictures and words to the teens takes a lot of the thought and creative process away from the children. I strongly feel it deprives the clients of making their own unique collage and digging a little deeper.

During graveyard shift we already go through literally hundreds of magazines pulling out inappropriate pictures. Plus, Ben always makes sure that the collages the residents present don't include anything inappropriate.

Sorry to be negative

Thanking you, Niki

Part of me believes what I write and part of me is merely way too lazy to cut out pictures all bloody night long. Lisa writes back that she had taken over 60 hours of art therapy classes and refuses to get into all of the therapeutic reasons as to why she is directing the project to be done in this manner. She further reprimands me for my "tone" and makes it quite clear that I need to follow her directives no matter how I feel about them.

Hmmm...well shit damn, Lisa. Following directives no matter what and without question sounds like lemming behavior, and we all know how lemmings end up.

Lisa's email reinforces my stance on *not* wanting to spend my nights cutting up magazines. I cut out pictures and words anyway, then sit silently seething at the next staff meeting when a 15-year-old girl proudly holds up her poster board and explains that she chose the pictures of a Chinese girl with pandas because it reminds her of herself and her love for animals. I know the picture comes from a National Geographic magazine and that it's a story about how giant pandas are a rare and very endangered species with only about 2000 left in the wild. From the magazine article I learned that pandas are considered a national treasure, and are used as the emblem of China, and that they spend 14 hours a day eating mainly bamboo. Had this client had the opportunity to see the entire article, she too, may have learned something. Instead she was now merely picking pictures that looked pretty. You feeing me, Lisa?

Lisa emails more directives for me to "follow" on my next graveyard shift. This time, I am to put together over 800 invitation mailers, which involves placing three different papers into an envelope in a specific order and then sealing the envelopes. On top of that, Lisa would like me to clean the shelter van parked outside.

I manage to put together a fair amount of the invitations, receiving several paper cuts to prove my diligence, but I refuse to go out in the middle of the night to clean the van. Plus, if I'm outside, the kids will be alone in the house.

"Screw you, Sandbag," I fume to the empty staff office. "You can shove your treats right up your bulky backside."

Since I have refused to follow Lisa's directive once more, I am hauled into head office to have a meeting with my superiors. I arrive nervous as hell, thinking maybe Sandbag has succeeded in getting me fired, which does seem to be her desired mission (and wouldn't be wholly unwarranted). However, when the headcheese (who hired Lisa) hears that Lisa wanted me to clean the van, stuff 800 mailers and do my regular duties as well, it is suddenly Lisa who is in the hot seat, not me.

I do not get fired, and happily, after several weeks, Lisa is informed that she is not a suitable fit for the shelter, and they let her go. Hah!

    Niki = One   Expressionless Sandbag = zero.

CHAPTER 23

Get a new Puppy

The Sandbag victory is a small triumph for my bruised (and embarrassingly childish) ego, and when Colleen is reinstated as shelter director, it helps me feel marginally positive about life. And then what do you know? Roy decides he is not completely finished with me after all. He reinitiates contact, and one wonderful dinner date later, our relationship quickly reverts back to *I want to see you* and *I now want you to disappear.*

It's farcical. We've officially been broken up for six months, yet still I'm like a confused bull with a ring pierced through my delicate nose. I follow his every command. If he calls for me, I rush to him. If he tells me to leave, I bawl all the way home. It's cruel, and I'm too feeble to stop it. I'm tethered to him yet I know I should put an end to this misery—cut the cord. Hack the cord. Slash the cord. Chew through it with my teeth if need be. But I simply can't. I ache to be with him.

Roy asks if he can come to one of my gigs. It's at Alta Coffee in Newport Beach, a cute, Avant-garde coffee shop. I suspect that the main reason Roy wants to join is because Brookie's parents (Mark and Arloa) will be there, and Roy likes the Moore family as much as I do. Roy feels connected to Arloa because they grew up in the same God fearing little town in Idaho (where evidently cinnamon rolls are hailed as some type of puffy paradise), and he gets along well with Mark.

Regardless of his motivations for joining, I'm wholly delighted that Roy is coming, but it's uncomfortable as hell playing guitar and singing knowing that he's sitting out there in the audience judging me.

I no longer know how to impress Roy. I no longer know how to be sexy in front of him. I no longer know anything.

Towards the end of my first set, as I finish a song, a beautiful man comes to stand before me. I can't even look at the man, that's how painfully aware I am that Roy is eagle-eyeing me. I can practically already hear Roy condemning me: "Look at her talking to strange men while she plays in a bar/coffee shop. She so lacks virtue. She just can't stop her slutty tendencies."

I further imagine that on a subconscious level, Roy's thoughts may be going something like this: "large penis threat in the house."

Hoping to circumvent any disapproval from Roy, I avoid eye contact with the man altogether.

"Would you teach me to play guitar?" Gorgeous man asks.

Yes, absolutely because—hubba-hubba.

"No, I don't really teach anymore." I say. "But I can tell you where to go for lessons." I don't even smile, I'm that rattled about upsetting Roy.

Gorgeous *does* smile, a winning, handsome smile at that.

"That's ok," he says. "I admire your style. I want to play like you. Tell you what, I'll put my phone number in your tip jar in case you change your mind."

Roy questions me the moment I join him at his table.

"Who was that guy?"

"Nobody."

"Did he put something in your jar?"

"A few dollars," I lie, aware of the handsome man's business card gleaming in my tip jar.

I don't really plan on calling this man, but I'm pleased that he placed his number in my jar because my shattered, battered ego is in dire need of a flattery boost. Yes, that is how I get my ego boosted— by men thinking I'm cute, or pretty, or sexy. What happens when I'm not? Probably another memoir, God help us all.

It's while my life is going down the toilet, that Roy gets the green light from Disney. And zim-zam-zoom, they start making his movie. This is a steady ego basher for me because now when Roy calls, all he can talk about is how great his life is. He has a new house. He has a new car. He has new friends and new admirers. The filming of his movie is going swimmingly. KC (one of the big stars in Roy's movie) has invited him for Thanksgiving. KC is taking him lobster diving. KC is hanging out with him at his ranch in Santa Barbara. Roy is travelling in private jets and limousines. His life is hunky-fucking-dory, and I sit and smile and nod and say: "I'm so happy for you, Roy."

And honestly, I really am. I'm happy for Roy that his lifelong dream is coming true. I'm actually glad that I get to be a part of it, no matter how miniscule my part is. It's a treat for me to hear the inside scoop of various celebrity meltdowns on location, the crazy behavior of some of the stars, the mishaps and calamities that happen on set. But the happier I am for Roy, the sadder I am for myself. Here I sit, hiding in a room of Tyrannosaurs and Raptors watching Roy receive everything he's ever wanted while my dream of having a singing career lies cold and dead in a dark corner. He's on set surrounded by fame and fans; I'm at the shelter surrounded by moody, oily-skinned teens. He's earning vats of gold; I'm earning fly droppings. He is excited and inspired; I'm heart broken and can barely muster up enough energy to climb out of bed in the morning.

Regardless, I smile, and smile, and never once think to say: "fuck you and your happy fucking life!" Which is what I should say, because honestly, how can I feel good about myself with his "joy" and "good fortune" constantly all shoved up in my face.

I strive to be upbeat and therefore force cheerfulness upon everyone I meet, stuck in that embarrassing stage where you overshare with complete strangers. You know, the stage where you're standing in the line at the post office and remark to the person ahead of you: "It's really hot in here, isn't it? Do you ever feel so lonely you think you might die?"

I can't stop myself—I'm a filter-less flibbertigibbet.

Me talking to a woman in the checkout line: "What do you think about singing in bars?"

Woman: "That's nice, sweetie...you sing?"

Me: "Or how about making cinnamon rolls? I suck at it."

Woman: "Uh, I've never tried."

Me: "How would you feel if someone insulted your vagina?"

Woman: "----------------". That's right. She's says nothing, because she's had the good sense to flee.

Fresh out of ideas and devoid of any self-worth, there coms a day when I drop to my knees in front of Roy and beg him to please, please, please give me another chance. My dignity has sunk to that of a squashed cockroach. It is depressingly degrading.

"Please, I'll do anything," I stare up at him, eyes full of tears. "Tell me what I can do to make this work with you?"

Roy pulls me off my knees and sits me on his lap. He hugs me tightly.

"I'm so sorry, Niki" he says. "I can't."

My anguish flows out into a song called "Worth it". It pretty much captures exactly what I'm going through.

I can't find a word to make myself heard
You simply cannot hear me
I would give my all, to break through your wall
But you don't want to be near me

CH: And I want to know, was it worth it, to let go

I struggle for a way to get through each day
I really feel quite broken
I've no will left in me, I should just let it be
'Cos you've already spoken

CH: But I want to know, was it worth it, to let go

It's all very well that I sing about Roy letting go of our connection, but I have to find a way to let it go myself. I can't keep going to him when he calls. I can't keep crying all the time. I can't spend my days waiting for him, thinking about him, desperate for him. Then it comes to me. I still have the phone number of that guy who dropped his card in my tip jar "in case I change my mind". That guy *liked* that I was playing a gig. He was fine with me performing in a bar/coffee shop. He thought my music was good. He seemed to like me.

Well, okay then, today is the day I change my mind. I rummage through my belongings to find the card that I know I've saved. Is this payback for Roy? Perhaps, but Roy probably won't care too much. I phone Dean anyway.

"Hi, yes. This is Niki Smart."
"Who?"
"The singer from Alta Coffee."
"Who?"
"You put your card in my tip jar."
God, I'm tragic.
"Niki! I'm so glad you called."
Okay, maybe not that tragic.

A short conversation has us set up to go on a date. Dean wants to take me to see "Chicago" and I find it a bit odd that this young man (younger than me by 8 years) wants to go see an old band like Chicago.

Of course, he doesn't. Dean has bought tickets to the musical show "Chicago" at the Pantages Theater in Los Angeles.

He goes all out to impress me. He books a dinner at a fancy French restaurant on Lido Isle where we eat goose liver and drink champagne. Then he drives us to LA, zipping in and out of the carpool lane, me liking him more each time he crosses those double, yellow lines— rules be dammed. God bless you, Dean.

Dean is everything Roy is not, and I thoroughly enjoy him. He is relaxed and spontaneous. He walks about barefoot and sings loudly (and unabashedly) in grocery stores. His beach apartment is full of sand and Star Wars paraphernalia, plus he has a huge comic book collection crammed into the bottom drawer of his desk, not photos of ex-girlfriends. He also has the largest speakers I've ever seen for in-home use. We listen to Dave Matthews, Lenny Kravitz, and The Killers, cranked up to "definitely-disturb-the-neighborhood" volume while we lie backwards on his bed with our legs up the wall. Dean grew up in Las Vegas where his father was a croupier, and because of this, Dean dislikes casinos and is not even slightly interested in gambling. To top everything off, Dean is <u>tall</u>, crazy hot, and has well-spaced eyes.

A few weeks into our courtship, we go for breakfast on the boardwalk in Newport Beach (yes, we have spent the night together). Sitting eating breakfast, I consider my situation. I'm seated next to a handsome, interesting man, my food is tasty, the view is fantastic, the weather is perfect, and yet I feel nothing but despair. In the corner, a couple smooch on each other passionately, and I have the notion that if they kiss one more time, I may have to slam my head into the table.

Tears prick my eyes as I frantically try to think of anything other than how much I miss Roy. Dammit. I really do like Dean, but I'm still in love with Roy, and there's nothing I can do about it.

Poor Dean. He puts in enormous effort. He burns me homegrown CDs of various artists whose songs I mention liking. He buys me tickets to see one of my favorite artists, Alanis Morrissette. He spoils me with dinners and attention. If he arrives early and I'm not ready, he simply says: "take your time, baby." He doesn't insult or criticize me. In fact, he compliments me endlessly and thinks I'm top notch. Even better, he thinks Samantha is top notch too, and includes her without me having to ask him to.

Come Valentine's Day, Dean shows up on my doorstep (well, Mark and Arloa's doorstep to be more accurate) with pre-made batter, syrup, strawberries and heart-shaped cookie cutters. Smiling his lovely smile, he proceeds to make me small pancakes in the shape of hearts. How frickin adorable is that? How lucky am I? Dean can't stay long though, because he has to get to work, and soon I'm alone with the remaining batter and strawberries. So what do I do? I gather up the ingredients, hop in my car and rush off to Roy's apartment. I show up on *his* doorstep offering to make him heart-shaped pancakes, as if the idea is mine, as if I bought the goodies, as if I possess such thoughtful and nurturing abilities.

Listen, it's not that I'm an awful human being, okay? It's biological …seriously. I've read about a study of heartbroken individuals who were still in love with their exes—and how they were still flooded with extra norepinephrine, which had them *more* in love, and *beyond obsessed*, and *extremely motivated to regain their lost love*. See? I can't help being tremendously driven to recapture Roy's love; that shit is in my bloodstream.

Here's the corker. MRI scans of these yearning lovers' brains showed neural pathways similar to the reaction a brain would have to a hit of cocaine, except they'd shifted slightly. Now the pathways were in the same basic regions as—wait for it—a compulsive gambler craving a big win. Good God! Roy (from Idaho) has become my own private casino.

I burn the pancakes and can't stop apologizing. I'm so nervous that I might appear unhinged that I appear utterly unhinged. It's not me, Roy—it's my bloody brain chemistry toying with my rational mind. My drive home from Roy's apartment sees me as heartsick as ever; I sob all the way home. Later that day, I receive an email from Roy. It lifts me up. It also rips into my heart.

Hello Nicola May
It was nice seeing you this morning…a bit painful as well. It's not easy to be reminded of what you are missing. You made my Valentine's Day. It was so nice to be able to squeeze you and dangle your feet. I miss you in my life. It was hard to say goodbye. It seems we've said good-bye a lot to one another. It never gets any easier. I hate when you leave. It underlines the silence I seem to live in. I thought of having you over for dinner. Reached for the phone a couple of times. Again, if there were anyone I'd want to spend Valentine's

Day with it would be you. You still reign supreme as my favorite human being. I've been listening to your song all day. You have such an incredible gift. I bow to your creative genius. I also hear the message of your song loud and clear. Was it worth it? Is this the right choice? Unfortunately, I still don't know the answer to that...to us. Would I like to see you tonight, or any night for that matter? Absolutely. Is it right to be with you without the promise of a future? No. Until I know the answer to that song with certainty...I don't think it's fair of me to be with you. I wish I had the answers, Niki. Believe me, I am trying to find clarity in my life. I truly want to do the right thing...whatever that might be. And I'm afraid seeing you without that clarity would lead us down a road we've already been. And I know you don't want to go there again. I think you were right....I have made a prison out of my life. And only I can tear down the walls I've built. And you of all people certainly don't deserve the incarceration I seem to dispense. Anyway...I'm babbling...sorry.

Just know this Nicola May. I do love you, and no matter what, you can always be assured that there is another soul out there in this world who truly cares about you. And I believe I have the same in you. Roy.

Hmmm, okay, so a few things. First, he almost makes it sound like I'm the one that has left him. Second, I must've played my "Worth It' song for him (good for me). Third, the promise of the future that Roy can't give me is the promise that he will marry me. He can't say that he will help me get legal status, so I don't have to worry, so that Samantha is safe, so that I can travel (I haven't left the country in over 12 years). What he *can* say is that he truly cares about me, and does love me; that I reign supreme as his favorite human being, but honestly, what is the point of that? Hearing how amazing he thinks I am just drills a deeper hole into my psyche. I'm a mess. I can't let go. I can't move forward. I'm solidly stuck.

Dean and I date for several months, me running to Roy whenever he calls and Dean unaware of my sidebar activity. Life with Dean is refreshing and revitalizing. Someone once said to me, "when your dog dies, buy a puppy", and without doubt, Dean is the happiest, most loving puppy I could have bought. His attention helps me enormously.

I grow to like Dean more and more, and just when I'm about ready to seriously consider taking things further with him, he sits me down for a talk. He takes hold of my hands, looks me in the eye and says, "Niki, I think we should stop seeing each other."

"What? Why?" I ask, the old familiar panic rising.

"I'm looking for a wife to have four kids with." Dean seems surprised that I haven't figured this out for myself. "Does that sound like you?"

To be honest, I'd completely forgotten that Dean was looking for anything. I was too busy focusing on a way to stay afloat. It hadn't entered my head that Dean was viewing me as a long-term solution when I was eyeing him as a handy-dandy quick fix.

I open my mouth to promise him four kids and a happy home life, but Dean is smarter than me. He puts his finger over my lips.

"I'll miss you," he says.

I'm floored. Dean was my back up guy. He was my replacement boyfriend. He wasn't meant to leave me, too. I'm sure that Dean sensed this—he's not stupid. Crap. My self-esteem was just starting to reboot, now I'm back to what a ghastly loser I am. Honestly, why *would* Dean want to date me? I'm obviously still in love with Roy, and even if that wears off, I'm not marriage material. I don't cook. I don't pop out offspring. I'm merely an aging, undocumented, poverty-stricken, wanna-be pop star. Would you want to take me out on a date?

Somehow, this second break-up pulls out all the stops. Down the spiral of self-loathing I plummet at a rapid pace. The momentum spins my brain into fits of senselessness. Desperate to gain Roy's attention, I make the first of many poor choices—I move to Corona Del Mar.

That's right, the very place I spurn for being shallow and plastic. The very place I mock fiercely and seriously look down upon. I move to Corona De Mar because I know that Roy hangs out at the Starbucks on the corner of PCH and Goldenrod Ave. He hangs out there almost every afternoon; therefore, CDM (Corona De Mar) suddenly seems like a most splendid place to live. In fact, three blocks from the Starbucks seems like the best spot on earth to rent an apartment. So I do. I rent a super-crazy-expensive apartment in CDM.

Oh boy. Save me, baby Jesus.

CHAPTER 24

Fight to the Death

My thinking has turned upside-down and inside out. I don't know who I am anymore. I don't understand myself at all. I'm all reactive and defensive, and I don't like who I am, or how I behave. On some level I KNOW what I'm doing wrong, but I simply seem unable to pull myself straight.

I know I dislike Corona Del Mar. I know I can't afford this apartment. I know I drink too much. I know self-worth doesn't come from looks (or from male approval). I know I find pretentiousness sickening, and yet here I am pretending more than most. I'm pretending not to be pretentious.

Corona Del Mar, population of roughly 14,000, median income of about $120,080 and 90% white = a vanilla suburb by the sea, stock full of folks with a sense of entitlement and much more money than class…oh, and me.

Roy frequents the Starbucks, and now so do I, in hopes of running into him. I sit amongst tittering, dolled up housewives and arrogant, well-groomed men who appear to have a set of unspoken rules unto themselves. One woman shows up every day in hip-hugging velvet sweats that brand her ass as ROXY. Her fingernails are French manicured, her makeup is L'Oréal model, her hair is lengthy luscious, her expression is deadpan. Apparently it isn't cool to smile when you're on display as a perfect specimen of female. I wonder about her. I wonder if she ever goes home and says to herself "Hell yes. That was a fantastically, awesome, shit-kicking day."

It distresses me that probably the only self-reflection she performs is viewing herself in mirrors. How will she ever truly enjoy her life? She's living a carefully constructed bubble-wrap life, a picture-perfect unblemished life. It makes me sad, but who am I to talk? I've ripped off every bit of my bubble wrap and now stand exposed, raw, and wounded. I can honestly say I am not enjoying my life at all.

Still, I sit at Starbucks surrounded by the erroneous enemy waiting in vain for Roy to show. By the way, I'm not a huge fan of Starbucks and prefer to support the mom and pop coffee shops, but at this point in my life, I'm completely out of alignment with the few principles that I have. I'm acting on panic-infused impulse. I've jeopardized my savings (and my sanity) all in the hopes of briefly seeing Roy at a coffee shop. That is pretty insane. And, of course, on the occasion that I do "bump" into Roy at Starbucks, seeing him doesn't help at all. He's not overly enthused to encounter me, and the minute he leaves, a typhoon of hopelessness swamps me. I feel rejected time, and time, and time again.

Although Roy is rejecting me, the rest of the men in Corona Del Mar seem to like me a lot. I'm followed home by an ageing man with a tragically bad toupee. It seems this sad-sack is prowling the neighborhood in his shiny sports car in search of some hot action. I think he thinks that I'm a hooker. Has he been talking to Roy?

Toupee man parks outside my house and begins peering in the windows. Samantha spots him first.

"Mom? There's a man with really nice hair trying to look in our windows."

I quickly draw all the curtains. What's this weirdo up to?

"Just ignore him," I say, and frown her way. "You think he has nice hair?"

Walking home from my daily Starbucks stakeout, a different man accosts me. This chump's in a sleek BMW that he slows to my walking pace, preventing me from crossing the street to my exorbitantly priced apartment. He winds his window down, does that leering "check you out" thing that yucky men do, and says "I'm the guy who walks his dog in your neighborhood."

"Huh?" I blink blankly at him.

"I'm the guy in the hood who walks his dog." He nods knowingly at me.

"Uh...ok"

"No, I'm the guy who walks his *dog*."

"I'm sorry, I don't know you."

"I'm the guy who walks his *dog*," he repeats, ogling me.

I don't know what he means. Where is this damn dog? Is it missing?

"Can you let me pass, please?"

I can't cross the road because if I step back, he reverses. If I move forward, he accelerates.

"The guy who walks his *dog*," he insists and ropes a wiry arm towards me.

Whatever Corona Del Mar cryptogram crap this is, I don't care. Fuck you and your dog, Mr. Creep-face. I spin around and bolt back to Starbucks.

The men's behavior in this area has me mystified until I discover that there is a prostitution racket going on in Corona Del Mar. Evidently, I fit the call-girl bill. I'm blonde, slender, have long hair and an accent. Since Americans tend to struggle with pinpointing accents, my South African accent could well be Czechoslovakian, which is where most of these poor girls hail from. I shudder at the thought of these old men cruising the streets in their fancy cars looking to prey on these young women who have limited means of survival. I feel for the girls. I understand their plight. Life can be a real stinky bitch.

Along with sympathy for the young women, a new sensation starts to percolate inside me. It takes a moment to surface and when it does, I realize it's anger—wild hammering anger. I'm angry at myself for being weak. Angry that I don't stand up for myself. Angry that I don't tell Roy to fuck off. Angry that the disgusting men in CDM think they can pay me to suck them off in their fancy fucking cars. Angry for many reasons. Holy saturated fat cow, I am definitely angry.

There is a saying that no matter how you squeeze an orange, orange juice comes out. Whether you slice it open, stick a straw in it, mash it, or smash it, orange juice comes out. Why? Because the goddam orange is full of orange juice, that's why. This saying is meant to illustrate how, if you're angry, no matter what situation presents itself, anger will come out of you.

It must be true because I scream at the girl at the front desk of my gym when she harmlessly asks to see my ID. Since I've left my ID at home, along with my ability to self-regulate, I go ballistic on her.

"I've been coming here for months," I yell at her. "I know you recognize my face. What horseshit is this? You think I'm trying to sneak in here?"

The poor girl's eyes widen as my anger blasts her, and mumbling an apology, she grants me entrance.

Great. I have bullied my way in. I have bullied her. I'm behaving like a spoiled Newport/CDM bitch.

On the treadmill, I sprint my anger levels back down to manageable, and soon regret my conduct. I shouldn't be yelling at the front desk girl. It's not her fault that I'm hurting. I head back to the front desk and apologize.

"I've just had my heart broken," I explain, hoping she'll understand. "I'm not in full control of my emotions yet. I'm sorry."

I have another undignified moment while waiting in a tediously long line outside a nightclub. Shirley and I've been waiting for ages to get inside when a group of scantily clad girls sidle up to the bouncer, wiggle and giggle, and he grants them access. I don't even know I'm upset until I'm shrieking in the bouncer's face. My anger hits at such a speed that my brain can't compute fast enough. I hurl all kinds of interesting obscenities at him, then stride away, my face dark red and on the verge of crying. What's my deal? How come I'm ready to go all raging bull on random strangers? Is it merely a safe outlet? A way to vent some of the building rage, frustration, and disappointment simmering within me?

Any little situation that "squeezes" me, angry, rancid orange juice comes out. Having lost control of my emotional self, I strive to have control over *something* in my life—anything. Thus, I fixate on stupid petty grievances and pump them full of my indignation. I dig in my heels with resolve for something that is of little consequence to me, or to anyone for that matter. Next time you come up against someone who is giving you strop about something seemingly insignificant, sit back a minute and ponder the reason why. Things are not always what they seem. And be warned—sometimes, in certain circumstances, people are ready to fight to the death for something ostensibly senseless.

11-year-old Hayley who enters the shelter with nothing but a backpack filled with her meager belongings, clearly illuminates this for me. Authorities find her on a bus and bring her to the shelter. Having been in and out of foster homes, Hayley, in her short eleven years on earth, has experienced twelve different placements in foster care. When things go south at these foster homes, Hayley ultimately bolts. This is how she came to be alone on a bus with her entire worldly possessions stuffed in her backpack. Her latest foster family has failed whatever test it was Hayley had set for them, and she'd fled.

Leading Hayley to her assigned bedroom, she clasps her backpack tightly. And no wonder. It really does hold her entire world. Imagine having everything taken from you. Your mother, your father, your siblings, your home, your friends, your school, and to make it worse, you have no control over any matters of importance in your life. You don't get any choice. You're simply shuffled around willy-nilly by a well-meaning but brutish system. Wouldn't you be fucked up? Wouldn't you be in deep crisis mode? Wouldn't you be in severe pain? Wouldn't you be vigorously pissed off?

Hugging her backpack, Hayley sits on the bed and stares out the window. Watching this grubby, tired ragamuffin clutching her tattered bag, it strikes me how very young she is. I can only imagine the trepidation she must be feeling being in a new place—yet again.

I bring her a warm washcloth and ask if she'd like to wipe her face.

"Thanks," she says, and dabs at her face, not quite capturing all the grime.

"May I?" I ask, and with her consent, clean the rest of the dirt off her face.

Her chin juts forward as she tilts her face up towards me. When I'm done, she stares hard at me with shiny eyes. "Could you give me a hug?" she asks.

Shelter rules forbid staff to touch the kids. It's for our own protection because, if I embrace a child and they misinterpret my action, they may claim I was trying to molest/abuse/assault them. We are allowed to briefly side hug and high five the kids. Nonetheless, if you had a terrified, beaten down little girl before you requesting a hug, wouldn't you want to take her in your arms and comfort her. Exactly.

I don't hesitate. I wrap my arms around Hayley's slight frame, and soon, she's shuddering against me as she silently cries.

"I think you're brave, Hayley." I praise her. "You're a very brave, young girl."

Unfortunately, things fall apart for Hayley pretty quickly. She makes it to Friday morning but then things explode. Reason being is that every Friday morning, the residents are scheduled to go on a hike. Since it is considered part of the shelter program, the teens *have* to participate unless they're not feeling well. In order to go on the hike, the teens are instructed to wear closed shoes. Hayley doesn't own any appropriate hiking shoes, but that's not a problem. Staff grab her some sneakers from the donation closet. Well, Hayley is not okay with wearing the donated shoes. She wants to hike in her own flip-flops (I understand because I like to hike in open shoes too—don't suffocate my feet, man).

Since Hayley's backpack houses the only things in the whole world that she *does* have a say over, these belongings take on enormous weight for her.

Staff explains to Hayley that she can't go on the hike unless she wears the sneakers; that her flip-flops are a liability for the shelter.

Hayley, in turn, explains to staff that she *is* going on the hike, and she *is* going to wear her flip-flops. She does this in fairly high-pitched voice because she is starting to escalate. Following protocol, as they are trained to do, staff calmly reiterate to Hayley that she can either wear the sneakers, or forget about the hike. I guess you know where this is going, because yes, a fight for your right to flip-flops can easily turn into a fight to the death.

If you have no say as to where you get to live, or with whom you get to live, you can bet your big bouncing bippy that saying which shoes you are going to wear (and where) takes on colossal import. Since the system has usurped Hayley's authority and left her powerless in the major decisions about her life, Haley reacts by investing all the clout she can muster into the minor decisions. The choice as to which shoes she can wear takes on an incredible significance for her. It is all she has left to fight for.

Regrettably, staff hasn't recognized Hayley's mindset—bear in mind that most of the shelter staff are in their early twenties, so they don't have a lot of life experience. They're doing what they believe is the right thing to do which means they don't back down, nor do they compromise.

Hayley, once again feeling like she is being pummeled by an unfair system, opts for a full-blown showdown. And what a showdown she delivers.

Not only does the poor girl scream until her vocal chords are cracked and raw, she furthermore hurls various pieces of furniture at staff, and barricades herself into her bedroom. As you know, shelter rules say we are not allowed to touch the residents, and we are most certainly not permitted to try and restrain them. If there is a problem with a resident, we dial 911.

When the police arrive, it takes four officers to get the raging, diminutive 11-year-old out of the shelter—and they have to hog tie her in order to do so.

I'm horribly upset when I read the log and find out what happened. I so wish I could've been there for Hayley. I'm convinced that I would have recognized her distress; that I could have intervened and saved the situation. I understand Hayley's rage. I understand exactly the intensity of having no one in your life that you can count on. No one that you can to turn to. No one that will help you, or go to bat for you. I know too well what it is to feel alone and unloved in the world. It's overwhelming and terrifying. And you can't help but scream and fight like a mad dog to endure. It's human instinct.

What's going to happen to Hayley? We haven't helped her. We pushed her to a showdown. We are ineffectual, feeble, pretend rescuers who simply talk-the-talk with no walk-the-walk follow through action. The system is so unfair. It bothers me. It irks me. It bugs and riles me. Yes, I'm fucking vexed. It troubles me to the point that I seek counsel from my director.

"Do we help these kids?" I ask Colleen. "I *need* to know. Do we make a difference?"

"Here's how I see it, Niki," she starts. "Even if these kids only catch a glimpse of normalcy, at least now they have something to measure their lives against. While at the shelter they experience what it's like to have three meals a day. What it's like to be in a place where there is no violence, no shouting, no insults, no unwanted sexual advances, no threats. They get to be in a clean, safe environment where they are treated with respect and dignity. Some of them have never experienced that."

I believe Colleen is right. The shelter does offer a glimpse of what a loving family might look like and act like. Perhaps, even the most dysfunctional, damaged teens can absorb this "positive environment" on some core level. I genuinely hope so.

Colleen further points out that our shelter was not the right fit for Hayley. If Hayley hadn't exploded today, it would have been tomorrow, or the next day. Hayley needs a long-term, group home placement, where she can hopefully get the counseling she needs before she turns 18.

Hayley, wherever you are, I hope you have found people to love and support you. I hope you have learned to love and support yourself. I hope for you. I really do.

I hope for me, too. I hope to learn to love and support myself. I've glimpsed a life of "comfort and belonging" except it was in Roy's arms, and I'm clueless as to how to make that happen for myself, without Roy. Images of Hayley screaming and hog-tied fuels my anger. I'm angry at a cruel world where little girls are abandoned. I'm angry at an unjust system that blindly steam rolls over human needs under the belief that it is providing for human needs. I'm angry at my life for not being what I want it to be. I'm angry that I am unable to help Hayley. But most of all I'm angry that I can't pull myself out of this rut.

Angry, angry, angry.

CHAPTER 25

Slap some Veneer on it

What to do with all this anger? I guess I should've paid attention during the anger management groups that we run at the shelter. What is it we teach the kids again? Not to focus on the negative, and to realize that "the world is not out to get you".

Oh yeah? Well, with Roy achieving his dreams while my life sucks and stinks, and stinks and sucks, it sure as hell feels like the world *is* out to get me.

How about this one? Try to realize when you are demanding something and change your demand into a request. Saying you would like something is healthier than saying you MUST have it. What? I don't understand. I MUST have Roy—and while I'm at it, Hayley MUST have a family. Why are we bothering the teens with this codswallop? I think my coping method for dealing with my anger is easier and way more effective. See you at the bar, kids.

Out drinking in a crowded bar, I'm being jostled about when someone elbows my drink into my mouth. The apparently rather sturdy wine glass hits my front tooth and chips it. Fabulous. Now I'm angry and ugly.

Having a fragmented front tooth leads me to make my second poor decision, which in all actuality, seems like a brilliant idea when it strikes. I decide to get veneers on my front teeth. Clever, right? Remember how Roy once mentioned my teeth being yellow during one of his critique sessions and suggested veneers? Well, if veneers make me look good to Roy, then Lord Almighty, I MUST have them.

Decision made—and honestly, I consider this to be pure genius at work. The next time I smile at Roy, he won't be able to push me away. He will fold. Veneers will win him back, n'est-ce pas? How can I fail with such ingenuity on my side? Yes, I'm criticizing the Corona Del Mar Roxy branded woman for her unrealistic and expensive facade only to want to procure one for myself.

I'm excited. I truly believe this is a game changer—six veneers on my top row of teeth. My million-dollar smile, or more accurately, my $5,000 smile, will knock Roy off his somewhat smallish feet—bada bing, bada boom. Talk about magical thinking.

I make an appointment with a dentist who specializes in veneers, or at least that is what her advertisement reads. Once I'm in the chair however, with five shots of epinephrine injected into my cheeks (giving me an overfed hamster look), I'm not convinced that this lady knows what she's doing at all. She files my teeth down into little, triangular-shaped, vampire fangs, then loosely places the specially "made-to-fit" veneers over my jagged remains. This is merely a rough alignment to test the waters, but she then unthinkingly hands me a mirror so I can judge for myself what these new shiners will look like.

My face has gone crazy puffer fish on me, my gums are soaked in blood, and the veneers sit askew permitting me a partial view of my freshly serrated gremlin chompers. One glimpse in the hand held mirror has me lightheaded. I'm going to pass out. I've paid $5,000 to transform myself into a nauseating freak show.

"I can't look at that." I say, and push the mirror away.

She apologizes and gets back to work, sealing the veneers in place. At this point, she's reading from a pamphlet and mumbling the instructions under her breath. I find this rather disturbing. Has she done this procedure before? I worry that I may be disfigured for life. Next time I see Roy, will I be smiling a mouth load of mutant horror at him?

No, actually—because my new veneers turn out wonderfully. They are a gleaming, uniform alignment of well-spaced spectacular enamel. I have the whitest teeth in…in…well, in all of my family for sure.

Roy is not enthralled by my new gnashers. What a shocker. He asks how much the veneers cost and tells me I better floss them regularly. It's a bit of a letdown, and as the air wheezes out of my unrealistic balloon, I realize what a dupe I am. Did I really believe I could win Roy back with fake teeth? Really? What kind of boondoggle nonsense did I convince myself into?

Not only that but I was so gung-ho to get veneers that I didn't research it adequately either. I didn't weigh up the pros and cons. I simply made an appointment, took out a loan, and opened wide. Now I owe $5,000, and have six teeth that don't quite match the rest of my "yellow" Chiclets.

A new kid at the shelter eyes my pearly whites during dinnertime.

"You have seriously white teeth," he remarks.

Tanner is a 17-year-old who entered the shelter after he attacked his grandfather with a bat. Tanner didn't actually strike his grandfather with the bat, but lifted it as if he were going to. Tanner's a big guy. I'm sure the grandfather got a hell of a fright. I'm even a little nervous of him.

"Thank you," I say, thinking it would be easy to lie about my teeth to the kids, but somehow I can't. It doesn't seem right. I expect them to tell me the truth. "I bought them last week," I confess, my face warming to bright red.

This gets all the kids attention and soon they're a tap, tap, tapping on my teeth.

"Those are fake?"

"How much did you pay?"

"Did it hurt?"

"Ok, that's enough," I say, my face on fire. "Let's clear the table."

When we've finished clearing dishes and doing kitchen chores, Tanner asks if he can talk to me.

"It's about these dreams I have," he says.

"Please, go ahead," I welcome him, glad that he is opening up and willing to share.

"I have two recurring dreams," Tanner starts. "They take place in the same setting, but have different endings. In the first dream, I'm at home and my family's asleep when a man breaks in through the window. He comes upstairs wielding a knife, planning to kill my whole family. I know he's there…and I surprise him by leaping out at him, and I shove him down the stairs. The fall knocks him out, so I tie him up, and I save my family."

"Sounds like a scary dream. How big is your family?" I ask.

"I live with my grandfather, his new wife, and my two younger sisters. My mother died of an overdose a few years ago, and my dad's in prison."

"That's tough. I'm sorry to hear that." No wonder the kid is struggling. "What's your second dream about?"

"It starts out the same. I'm at home and everyone is sleeping. The same man breaks in with his knife, but this time, I somehow become that man and I kill my entire family. I stab them all to death." Tanner looks at me expectantly.

Oh shit. Tanner murders his whole family.

"That's a pretty disturbing dream to have," I say, my mind searching for an appropriate response (other than: okay, time to go).

"Thank you for sharing that with me," I add. "I think it's important you tell your therapist about your dreams, too." Yup, extremely important. Très important. Muy importante. Sehr wichtig.

Tanner does tell his therapist and, following his session, she assures staff that, "Tanner wouldn't hurt a fly." Oh yeah? Tell that to his grandfather. Would he agree? Aren't Tanner's oneiric tales about a very real battle going on inside himself? In one dream, he is the hero; in the other he is the killer. To me that speaks volumes about his state of mind, and it's clearly not completely stable. I wouldn't be so quick to throw out an avowal that: "Tanner wouldn't hurt a fly." Me thinks he may be capable of supreme violence. Tanner is like my new teeth—perfect looking on the surface while underneath lurks a jagged horror.

164

Luckily, the therapist appears to be right on this one because Tanner doesn't hurt anyone while in our care. And fortunately for his grandfather, Tanner doesn't return home. His therapist makes arrangements for Tanner to join Job Corps—a no-cost technical training program administered by the U.S. Department of Labor that helps young people ages 16 to 24. A good chunk of our teens end up going to Job Corps. It's perfect for teaching young people the skills they need to become employable and independent, plus it helps place them in meaningful jobs. Hooray for Job Corps.

Dreams can be quite illuminating, can't they? I have a pretty revealing dream myself. In my dream, I'm with Samantha and we're trapped. Our only hope of escape is to swim across a huge swimming pool. The swimming in itself isn't a problem. The problem is that the pool is full of thick, brown, pestiferous muck. I realize it's going to be nearly impossible to make headway, and sinking into the sludge, it hits me. We are swimming in shit. Masses and masses of shit.

Not hard to decipher what's up in that dream. Samantha and I are in shit and it's going to take super human effort to swim through said shit. No wonder my mind has chosen a swimming pool because that's the one place where I've always felt safe. I loved to swim underwater as a kid, because underwater was the one place where no one could see me, touch me, or yell at me. Once submerged in my "liquid sanctuary" I could temporarily escape my mother's constant despair.

Well, now my liquid sanctuary is heaving with excrement, and to make it worse, my young daughter is stuck in it with me.

Samantha deserves better.

CHAPTER 26

Missing

It's been several months and I'm not getting better. I'm down sliding into a dark place, smiling the whole time, pretending to be fine. Isn't that what humans do? Thank you, I'm fine...yes, perfectly fine. Would you mind helping me tighten this noose around my neck? Because in reality, I'm suffering my ass off—like a new acronym: SMAO, or better yet, ROFS—rolling on the floor suffering.

The thought crosses my mind that it may have been easier on me if Roy had died. Had he passed away, people would have huddled around me, brought me casseroles and comfort, and sanctioned my wallowing in sorrow. They would have been patient with me, supported me, looked after me. Instead, I can't let people know how heartbroken I still am. They'll think I'm puerile, or self-indulgent. And the fact that I still run to Roy whenever he calls, that *is* my fault—maybe I don't deserve any pity. Perhaps I am bringing this all on myself?

I wonder what that shelter staff would think if they knew how outlandishly I've been behaving? Thank God they don't know. How could they? I present a whole different Niki when I'm at work. While at the shelter, I'm together, sensible, grounded. I actually pride myself on being able to accurately recognize when residents are escalating, and on my ability to calm them down quickly. Believe it or not, I'm at my best in crisis moments. I stay calm and my brain thinks clearly. How come I can do for the teens what I am apparently unable to do for myself?

On my next shift, I'm told to shadow Nathan. Nathan is on a strict one-on-one watch because his best friend recently committed suicide and Nathan is taking it very hard. Someone must be at Nathan's side at all times. I almost envy the kid. I'd like someone assigned to my side at all times. I feel in need of constant supervision myself.

Nathan asks to use the restroom and adhering to our one-on-one protocol, I wait outside the bathroom door. I hear Nathan tinkling. I hear the toilet flush. I hear a scraping sound that I recognize as the window opening. I know that window leads to the roof. I knock on the door. No answer.

"Nathan?" I call out. Silence.
I try the door. It's locked.

"Nathan, open the door, please," but I know he isn't going to. I've brought the "special" key with me and quickly unlock the door. "I'm coming in," I call out a warning, in case he's doing his business. But the bathroom is empty. Nathan has climbed out the window.

"Nathan's on the roof!" I yell down the stairs and hastily clamber out the window myself.

Nathan stands near the edge of the roof.

"Hey Nathan," I say. "Let's go back inside."

Nathan doesn't look at me. He's staring at the street two stories below. Beneath us, on the road, a group of local kids on skateboards perform tricks. Suddenly, the smallest of the group, an angelic, long blonde-haired, typical surfer kid spots us and nudges his buddies. The group gazes up, and the angelic one yells: "Jump, you big pussy."

They all snicker and I'm speechless. Little fuckers. Who does that? Spoiled little, Newport Beach brats with zero empathy. Pimply sociopaths in the making. I hope the universe sees fit to dole out some major road rash to them all.

Pleased with themselves, the gang jauntily thread away on their skateboards while Nathan screams a healthy "fuck you" after them, and bursts into tears. Placing an arm about his shoulders, I say, "Let's go back in the house". Thankfully, he complies.

Back inside, my hands start shaking and an intense craving for a glass of wine hits me. Am I shaking because I need booze, or because

Nathan's suicidal endeavor unnerved me? Or was it the heartlessness of the other kids? Whichever, the rest of my shift is spent plotting when and where can I get a drink? It's horrible to admit, but I realize that right now I don't care that much about Nathan, or the other kids for that matter. I'm much more worried about me. The kids are still young. They have plenty of time to work on their issues. They've made it to the shelter. That's a good start isn't it? Whereas me? I'm a fraud working at a shelter, pretending that I can help others though I feel like jumping off a roof myself. What am I doing here? How am I helping these kids if I don't have enough energy to care about them? I don't even have the energy to care about my own daughter, or me. I'm fucking depleted. Worn out. Exhausted. The thought of what a useless parent I'm being for Samantha quadruples my desire for a drink. I just can't deal with anything right now.

    I try to at least contest my longing for wine. Do I really want to go out and drink myself to death? That won't help in the long run. Don't I want things to change? I need to change. I recognize that, right? Nathan didn't jump off the roof. He made the right decision. Surely I can, too? Yes? Please yes?

I promise to remain conscious of my consumption. I won't simply go out and get obliterated; I'll just take the edge off. To ensure my success, I select my new friend, Deborah to go out with. She's not a wild drinking girl like Shirley. Deborah's stable. This will be good. My plan is to go and enjoy *one* glass of wine…okay, possibly two, but that's it.

    No big surprise here, but I'm quickly on my second glass of wine at a crowded bistro, shoving French fries in my mouth. I notice an old flame of mine across the room and excuse myself from Deborah. I weave my way through the sweaty throng towards him, glass of wine in hand, sipping on my drink as I meander.

    Then, all of a sudden, I completely disappear. My last memory of the night is of zigzagging through that crowd towards my ex (he's the one with the large apparatus, not that that's in any way relevant).

I resurface seven hours later in the back seat of an SUV, totally confused. Where's Deborah? Where's the restaurant? Where am I?

I glance out the window unable to compute what I'm seeing.

"Is this Corona Del Mar?" I wonder stupidly.

My body feels wrong. I'm in an ungainly position on the back seat of a strange car. My neck's twisted around and it hurts when I lift my head to look out the window. My legs are at odd angles. My brain feels wrong. I'm used to being drunk, I know how that feels. This is different. I can't wake up properly—as if I'm trapped in a lucid dream. I know I'm awake, but my brain is thick, murky—not fully conscious.

My pants feel wrong. There's a wad of material bunched up at my knees under my jeans. I slide my hand into my pants and realize it's my underwear, tightly rolled up and stretched beyond what any underwear should endure. And what the hell is this sticky thing adhered to my thigh? I peel off a lightly soiled sanitary napkin. Oh, that's just dandy.

I'm still trying to figure out where the restaurant is, how I got here, and why I feel so drugged, when a man's voice says, "Lucky you're on your period or I *would* have raped you."

It's not a voice I recognize, and the tone is absolutely not friendly. It's threatening. A prickle of fear quivers through me, urging me to sober up. Wake up, Niki. Please wake the fuck up. Craning awkwardly towards the driver's seat, I decipher the silhouette of a muscular mountain of a man. I can only see the back of his gleaming, bald head, and a bulging arm inked up with tattoos. His skin is smooth, dark. Possibly he's Mexican, I can't tell, but I have no idea who he is, or how come I'm in the back of his SUV. My brain can't assimilate the information. It simply can't. My mind's awash in swamp mud.

"I have to go," I rasp out, my voice hoarse and unfamiliar, and grabbing the door handle, I clumsily topple out of the car.

On recognizing a building nearby, I beeline to it. Some part of my brain is obviously still working because I know I *must* get away from this man as quickly as possible.

I spot a dark alleyway near the building and bolt to it. Squeezed behind a dumpster, I breathlessly watch the car. Bald-mountain sits still in his white SUV. It doesn't dawn on me to read his number plate, and in my Quaalude like state, I doubt I'd be able remember any combination of letters or numbers anyway. I pray that he will drive away, and thank you God, eventually he does.

Pumped full of adrenaline, my heart pounds sickeningly hard. I'm lightheaded. I actually cannot walk for fear of passing out, so I crawl. I crawl along PCH with my underwear bunched at my knees. I can't figure out how to uncurl my undies and I don't really care at this point. I don't care if anyone sees me, either. I'm way beyond all that. All I care about is getting home and locking the door firmly behind me.

I've never been so glad to see my expensive apartment. I collapse though the doorway, slam the door shut, and bolt it securely. Thank God, Samantha is spending the night at a friend's house. I'd hate her to have to witness me in this state.

Thinking of Samantha sends me over the edge. Whimpering animal sounds mewl out of my throat—sounds I've never made before. Glancing sideways in the hall mirror, I gasp at my reflection. I'm unrecognizable. My hair is a snarled rat's nest. Makeup and grime smear across my face. My eyes are puffy, purple slits. Have I been beaten?

I crawl into bed, and though it's a hot summer night, I start to shiver. I tug on an extra blanket but still can't get warm. I curl into a ball, my body shaking violently. I rock back and forth whispering over and over to myself: You're ok. You're ok. You're ok.

But I'm not. I'm in shock.

I wake with a burst of terror and desperately want to call Roy. I need someone to calm me, reassure me. The bright sunlight streaming through the windows does nothing to suppress my fear. Overnight, the world has transmuted into a frightening and dangerous place.

From my cell phone, I can determine that I went missing at roughly 9 p.m. That's when Deborah texted me "where are you?"

Several more texts from her end at around midnight with: "Ok. Call me when you can."

Receipts in my purse place me at three different bars. My signature is a vague chicken scratch scrawl. I'm not even sure that I signed them. Did I? I have to pull myself together. Samantha is coming home. She can't see me like this.

I clean myself up but can't shake the feeling that something is wrong, wrong, wrong. In my mind I feel like I was kidnapped. What if mountain man is doing this to other girls? What if he does something to one of the kids at the shelter? He's probably roaming the neighborhood in his white SUV right now, and holy shit—he knows, more or less, where I live. What if he harms my daughter? That thought terrifies me. I drive to the closest police station.

It's humiliating.

The police ask, "How often do you drink?"—umm, all the time.

"How much do you drink"—uh, plenty actually.

"Have you blacked out before?"—well...yes. Yes indeed. But officer, this time it was different.

And it was different. This time I wasn't drinking in my usual slug/chug/glug style. I was being careful. Did I really just black out? Surely not? I mean, I didn't *want* to get drunk. Am I that far gone in the drinking game that I black out after two drinks and stay blacked out for seven hours? I refuse to believe that. I believe I've been drugged. I believe I've been roofied.

It's hard to convince the police, though. Nevertheless, they visit the three drinking establishments that my receipts hail from and diligently sift through all their video surveillance tapes. I am nowhere to be seen at any of the places.

They send a policeman to my apartment to collect evidence: my used sanitary napkin. It may have mountain man's DNA on it. I fish the soiled pad out of my trashcan and hand it to the officer, my face burning bright red.

It's illuminating.

The female officer assigned to my case asks me to come in for a follow up session. She inquires if I have noticed anything different since the incident.

I have. I have noticed that my body starts to shake involuntarily whenever a dark skinned, bald man approaches. The same thing happens whenever a white SUV passes me by on the street. The officer explains that though my brain cannot remember what happened to me, my body can. It's called cellular memory. She further explains that this reaction from my body suggests that my body sensed it was in danger. She believes I felt threatened on a deep level.

She further enlightens me to the fact that the brain cannot make memories while blacked out.

"It isn't that you can't recall what happened to you," she tells me. "There is no memory in your brain for you to access."

Okay, so I will never remember what happened that night. Perhaps that is a blessing in disguise.

I must stop drinking. I'm too vulnerable when I'm drunk. I leave myself wide open to…to…to anything out there. And maybe I wasn't roofied? Maybe that was just my brain melting down after months of heavy alcohol intake. Next time, I may not wake up. What would happen to Samantha then? Would she go and live in Cape Town with her father that she has only met once? Pouring alcohol into myself during this frail period is a bloody rotten idea. I need to be sober. I need to get clear.

Yes, basically I'm scared straight. Well, nearly.

CHAPTER 27

Destitute

I make it in to staff meeting, although my mind is not focused on work. I'm not in my right mind at all, so when our newest client, 14-year-old Fiona, stands up to read her "This is Me" with bandages on both her forearms and multiple angry scabbed slashes across her face, I imagine she's been attacked by some heinous man. Is the world simply full of brutal, scary men now?

No, actually.

Turns out Fiona's wounds are self-inflicted. After slashing up her face, Fiona slashed open her wrists and was rushed to the emergency ward. Once stitched, stapled and stabilized, she was funneled to our shelter.

In my macabre state of mind, I'm fascinated by Fiona's visage. It's unusual for teens to cut their faces. I figure Fiona may have some excessive self-loathing going on and is aiming to disfigure herself? Maybe she feels so ugly on the inside that she wants the outside to match? Perhaps she wants others to visibly witness her pain?

Most cutters feel ashamed of their wounds and strive to hide them, which is why inner thighs and underarms are popular sites for cutting. Slicing open her face may be a sign that Fiona is ready to get help? It could well be a loud, grisly call for help.

"My name is Fiona," she says flatly. "I'm fourteen years old and live with my mom and her new boyfriend. I came to the shelter because I cut up my face...and my wrists." She pauses, rustles her paper, and stares fixedly at Colleen. "I can't answer this next one 'cos I don't have anything that I'm proud of."

Colleen jumps in to help her. "Is it hard for you to be reading your 'This is Me' to us?"

Fiona nods.

"Well then, be proud of yourself for doing that, because you're doing it." Colleen nods reassuringly.

Fiona squints at our director and tries on her advice. "I'm proud of myself for reading my paper out loud to staff today."

Staff gives her a round of applause as encouragement but Fiona doesn't react. She remains expressionless. "When I leave the shelter I hope to not want to kill myself anymore."

Seeing as over 75% of our clients are referred to the shelter following suicidal thoughts or attempts, "not wanting to kill oneself anymore" is not an uncommon goal for our residents. These teens attempt suicide in a myriad of ways. We've had kids who've tried by to kill themselves by swallowing masses of Tylenol, jumping off balconies, slashing at their wrists. One young man wrapped a vacuum cleaner cord about his neck, another jumped out of a moving car—mostly however, these attempts are not too severe. These kids don't want to die. They want to be loved. Their suicidal efforts are an absolute cry for help, and I'm glad that here at the shelter, we can at least try to offer these children the beginnings of that help.

Skirting dangerously close to being suicidal myself, I wonder what the hell I'm doing working at a facility that deals predominantly with children in crisis. I'm a hazard. I should "turn myself in".

The reason for the upsurge in Fiona's cutting comes to light. Fiona is pregnant. Wait, it gets way worse. Fiona is pregnant from her mom's new boyfriend.

We are not the right facility to help Fiona and so she's sent to wait out her pregnancy at a safe house for young expectant mothers. The mom's new boyfriend is sent to jail.

"Let's cut on him," I'm thinking. "Let's cut on his testicles with razor blades".

Soon after Fiona exits, 16-year-old Dianna enters our shelter. This teenage girl has been living in a car with her mother for the past 8 months. They tried moving in with friends but the mom inevitably got into a fight and things rapidly soured. The mom has outstayed and out-argued every available resource.

On entering the shelter, Dianna is extremely guarded. She's reserved, doesn't interact with the other residents, complies with our rules but basically keeps to herself. She's also extremely bedraggled. Her clothes are worn-out and her dark hair is dank with oil and smells funky. Smelly kids are pretty normal at the shelter—lots of our teens struggle with hygiene and we have to hound them to shower. We don't have to hound Dianna, though. She asks to shower right off the bat.

"It's wonderful to have fresh smelling hair again." She says inhaling on her long black hair.

Once Dianna realizes her stay at the shelter is for real, she does an about-face and blossoms.

Dianna is lovely. She's smart, funny, and considerate. With her new confidence in us, she becomes chatty and willing goes above and beyond in helping with any chores. She's patient and kind to the other residents, even Robbie, a 12-year-old autistic boy who drives us all crazy with his never ending questions. Robbie keeps inquiring if Diana would like to watch him control his breath, which he claims he can hold for 4 minutes (he can't), and he's further fascinated by her ample breasts and requests to know her bra size almost every hour. Diana tells him good-naturedly, "It's the same size as your brain."

Dianna's happy to be at the shelter and asks to stay longer than her 32 days. She doesn't want to go back to living in a car.

"I like having a bed, and a closet for my clothes, and being able to shower whenever I need. And the food is so awesome here."

Dianna is an exemplary client...that is until the time draws close for her to leave the shelter. Knowing that she has to return to her mom and the car, Dianna regresses back to sullen and non-responsive. She stops showering and withdraws. The night before she's meant to exit the shelter, Dianna goes to bed super early in a piss-poor mood. Can't say I blame her.

I'm on graveyard shift and have been instructed to watch her throughout the night as she's considered a flight risk. I clock in, read the log, and make sure Dianna is the first person I check on. I knock gently on her room door.

No answer—she could be asleep, it is already 11:30 p.m. and I can hear soft music playing (the teens are given CD players and are encouraged to listen to music that has been approved by a staff member—no profanity or violent/sexual lyrics). In my gut though, I know before I open the door. Dianna's bed is empty and the window is wide open. Dianna has run away.

In case you're wondering why we don't have alarms on the windows, we do. Dianna has managed to disarm the alarm. I told you, she's smart.

I call the police.

They arrive at the shelter and I give them our photo of Dianna. We take photos of our residents the day they come in—yes, we're smart, too.

"We have an APB out on her," the officer says. "We'll find her pronto."

I call Dianna's mother.

"Hi Melinda. This is Niki from the shelter."

"Yes?"

"I'm sorry but Dianna has run away. We've called the police and they are out looking for her right now."

"That stupid girl." The mom groans into the phone. "What am I supposed to do? Does she think I have money for gas to drive around looking for her? I barely have enough gas to pick her up." The mom lets out a huge sigh and hangs up.

Within an hour the mom shows up at the shelter, which is surprising, as she's just stated how she barely has the gas to get here. I brace myself, fully expecting her to make a grand old scene—to yell, to cry, to throw a hysterical shit-fit—but no, on the contrary.

"Everything is fine," she smiles radiantly at me. "I phoned my boyfriend in Australia and he's on his way here to help me look for Dianna."

176

Uh…what? That's a 15-hour flight not counting all the other rigmarole that goes along with traveling. How does that make everything okay?

"Is he close with Dianna?" I ask.

"He hasn't met her yet," the mom says brightly.

I don't know what to say. I'm not sure I understand exactly what is going on here. The mom soon fills me in.

"We've been dating online." She crows, giddy with excitement. "It will be my first time meeting him, too."

Uh…WHAT?

Oh Dianna. You poor, poor girl.

The police find Dianna at 5 a.m. running through someone's backyard and briefly bring her back to the shelter to gather up her belongings. Dianna stares past me the whole time, refusing to make eye contact, uncommunicative and morose.

I recognize both Dianna and Fiona. I recognize them as young girls who've had their hearts broken, their dreams crushed, their inner most needs overlooked. Their disappointment is palpable. They look defeated.

I'm not sure how much more heartbreak I can bear to witness.

CHAPTER 28

What goes up must come down (and vice versa)

The teens at the shelter are good kids saddled with unfair and, oft times, horrific circumstances that they don't deserve. I can't make sense of it. How does the universe decide who gets what? Why are some born into a loving family, or into money, or good looks, while others get a perpetual address on shit-street?

Life seems particularly unfair at this moment, and of course, right as my world crashes down around me, everything starts coming up roses for Roy. His movie is ready to hit the circuit and Disney shouts its much-anticipated arrival from the sides of buses, up high on billboards, and splashed all across magazines and newspapers.

Everywhere I look, Roy's success slaps me in the face, stings my heart, and douses me in envy and sorrow. How desperately I want to be at Roy's movie premiere in Los Angeles. I ache to walk on the red carpet alongside the man I love.

How am I supposed to comfort the kids at the shelter? I can't tell them everything will be okay. I can't assure them that their parents do love them. I can't promise them a joyful future or even a shot at a joyful future. Life seems bleak...but I can't tell them that either.

Unable to comfort myself, I make my final bad decision and do the very thing I've recently promised myself I wouldn't do again.

Yes sir, you are correct. The night of Roy's premier, I go out and drink, drink, drink and drink like there is no tomorrow. At this rate, there may well be no tomorrow. I know, I know—I'm annoyed, ashamed and astounded by my behavior, too. Didn't I just say that bucketing alcohol into my system right now can only lead to a bigger shit-show? Mountain man was a wakeup call. A big bald warning.

Why am I not paying heed to el hombre? I'll tell you why. Because I'm too sad, too tired, too fucking destroyed to stomach being sober. All I can think to do is drink.

And drink I do. I go out and get so magnificently plastered that I black out and wake up in my car. This is the time I wake up in an underground parking bay, bruised up in my passenger seat with my clothes unbuttoned, my hair falling out, and my glasses and coat missing. This is the time I foul up my car seats with menstrual blood, and slink home to lie in my lonely, singlewide bed whispering to myself "I no longer want to be alive."

I lie staring up at the ceiling, my body bloated and tender, my head spinning, my heart hammering erratically. Is it even possible to sink any lower? I couldn't feel any worse than I do right now. I'm experiencing the nadir of my existence (or at least it feels that way). There is no joy in my day. There is no joy in my life. I live in an area that I despise, in an apartment that I can't afford. I've veneered myself into serious debt. I've sunk into a relentless depression. I've devolved into a disengaged parent. I'm drinking my health into the toilet. I'm jeopardizing my welfare, and that of my daughter. I'm making zero headway in my musical calling while Roy's career is skyrocketing. Roy is flying in private jets and riding in limousines. I'm blacking out and coming perilously close to being raped in SUVs.

This is it—rock fucking bottom. I'm broken in every way: physically, emotionally, spiritually and financially. I am 100% miserable. This is not life. This is more like torture. No longer being alive doesn't sound that bad.

While wallowing in my gloom, a thought arises. If this is me, bottoming out at my lowest point, that means that I have nowhere to go but back up again, right? Maybe this is a turning point? This notion offers enough relief to allow me to sink into a black sleep. I wake up already crying and force myself to get up, get showered, and get dressed. I cry the entire time. I cry the entire day. No wonder. When your body is full of toxins from major alcohol consumption, your brain doesn't think lovely happy thoughts. No, it's swarming with destructive, fear-riddled, doomsday thinking.

Finally, my hangover wanes and I sit myself down to write up a list. I title it: "Things to do". Not very imaginative, I know, but creativity is hard to muster when you're at zero. I simply list all the steps I'll need to take in order to climb out of this black hole. I have to find a way to get back on my feet. First off, what's the point of living in Corona Del Mar in the hopes of bumping into Roy when he has no intention of being with me and I can't afford my rent? It's absolutely senseless.

With my stomach in distressed knots, I confess to my landlords (an elderly Christian couple) that I can't manage my rent. I tell them that it's crushing me, and ask if they will please, please, please, with a multitude of cherries on top, let me out of my lease? Naturally, being good Christian folk they say no—because charity starts at home and sometimes it doesn't make it out the front door.

Fine. Then I shall blame them for forcing me to conjure up a lie that involves a terminal illness.

After receiving my lengthy, lying letter, they acquiesce, but they keep my full deposit and demand another month's rent. It's a whopping amount and I vehemently begrudge their Christian asses for squeezing money out of me. I fork over my savings because I'm red-hot to escape my horrendously high-priced apartment, and the wasteland that is Corona Del Mar.

Samantha and I move to a much more affordable studio apartment right across the street from her high school. We divide up the tiny 500 square foot studio apartment and jokingly call out to each other: "I'm in the bedroom" or "I'm in the living-room".

A walk-in closet serves as the TV room. The kitchen counter functions as both the dining table *and* the study. Most of our belongings are stored in cardboard boxes out on the balcony covered with a plastic tarp.

We're basically living on top of each other, but we do it fairly well. This new location is perfect for me as I no longer have to drive Samantha to school, and driving Samantha to school has always proved to be an insurmountable task for me. Poor Samantha, she's had to bike to school, walk to school, or catch the bus to school, all because I'm not a morning person. You try drinking all night and then getting up early to drive a kid to school. What's that? Maybe I should stop drinking? Are you crazy?

Our new studio apartment is perfect for Samantha too, because now she is right across the street from the action. I tell her "This is your last year of high school, Manthy. Make the most of it. Make it a year that you can one day look back on with fondness."

Samantha rolls her eyes at me like I know nothing. But I do know. I know the other side. I left school at 15 and therefore didn't get to go to a school dance, or have a graduation party. I have no fond high school memories and I really wish I did. I wish I could've stayed in school and been able to focus on schoolwork and school life, but I was too busy focusing on merely surviving.

The eye roll must have been for show because Samantha evidently does hear me. Next thing I know her "school spirit" kicks into high gear and soon she's involved in all kinds of after school activities. She's part of a mentoring program for new kids arriving at high school called "Freshman Seminar". She puts together a team to run in the school marathon, going so far as to make T-shirts for her teammates. She attends several school dances that up until now were considered pitiful. She embraces her school and I'm thrilled. Look at Samantha having a somewhat "normal" childhood.

"Hey child of mine, I'm in the TV room!"

The other bonus of moving to this tiny home base is that it's way easier for me to pay my rent. With this decrease in financial stress, I relax slightly, and cut back on my hours at the shelter. Fewer graveyard shifts are paramount because, on top of everything, the irregular sleep patterns formed by staying up all night have messed with my hormones and my adrenal glands—and honestly, who wants to be a palpitating, bloated, hormonal mess? Maybe if I can heal my body, my mind will follow? Maybe I can find a better antidote then alcohol? Maybe I can find a way to stop Roy's face-voice-body-laugh playing on a repeat cycle in my brain? Maybe I can rise up from rock bottom?

CHAPTER 29

Flip Switch

It's probably fairly obvious from my drinking patterns, that I'm kind of extreme. If I'm going to do something, I'm going to go the whole hog-wild way. This immoderation works in my favor when I commence a journey into myself. Attention—Achtung—Atención. I'm going in deep, people. I will unflinchingly dig and scrub and slosh around in the depths of me/myself/I until I find relief.

I refer back to my "Things to do" list, check off #1: *less expensive apartment* and move onto #2: *Enroll in yoga classes and swim more*.

I used to do yoga but stopped because the classes became too pricy. However, I know that yoga can relieve stress by calming and centering the nervous system—and yes please, I need that. Once back in the yoga-zone, I remember that I LOVE yoga. I can't get enough of it and practice whenever I can.

Check that one off the list.

Another bonus is that our new apartment comes with a huge swimming pool hence I spend as much time as possible underwater — that's right—'tis my liquid sanctuary and it serves to relax me.

It occurs to me that at the shelter, we've helped kids in way worse situations than mine. Seeing as I've been behaving like an out-of-control teenager, why don't I try to follow the routine we implement for our clients? What would I do with me if I were admitted to the shelter? Hmm, well—the teens start their day by going for a power walk. Fine, let's buy me some running shoes.

And whaddya know? My power walk turns into a gradual jog, along with the discovery that running helps soothe my anxiety levels when they're spiking into the stratosphere. Just being outside in the fresh air helps soothe me. I research what it is about fresh air that is so invigorating and find out that it's thanks to negative ions. These little guys are abundant, especially near water. This may explain why we feel peaceful near the ocean, or waterfalls, lakes, and si señor, swimming pools.

And guess what? Negative ions can affect the serotonin levels in the brain, making fresh air and exercise an effective treatment for depression.

Excellent.

I shall run on the beach, I shall run by river. I shall boost this here mood of mine. Boost, boost, boost.

This is good stuff. What else do we make the kids at the shelter do?

1. *They are only allowed limited sugar.*
Okay, that's not too hard. Done—no more sugar.
2. *They don't drink caffeine.*
That's not as easy, but big groan, and—done. No more coffee.
3. *They don't drink alcohol.*
Dammit. Dammit. Dammit—working on that one.
4. *They exercise.*
Marvelous, I'm running, swimming and doing yoga. Nailed it.
5. *They set daily goals.*
No problemo, I can do that. Today my goal is to do whatever the teens at the shelter do.
6. *Lastly, they journal.*
Hot-diggity-dog. I could write a whole book (you may have noticed). Done.

I journal pages and pages of self-reflection, determined to pen some of the poison out of my soul. I devour every self-help book that crosses my path. I read and read, convinced that I will find an answer to my despair somewhere on the pages.

One day, while tidying up the recreation room at the shelter, I come across a book called "Letting Go" by David Hawkins. I open the book to a random page and start reading and everything I read resonates with me—deeply. It's like this book has been written specifically for me. Oh, I must have. Must have.

I sneak the book into my bag. My new procurement is all about the title—letting go. That simple—that complex.

Here's the gist of it more or less:

1. First, notice what you are feeling without judgment – *I'm feeling fucking terrified, thank you very much, and have done for about two years now. I'm seriously exhausted.*
2. Sit with the feeling, don't try to solve or repress it. Just allow it to be—*Oh, it's being all right. It's being sheer panic sitting heavily on my chest.*
3. Then let it go—*Huh? Wait! Explain like you would a child.*

It takes me several re-reads to absorb the information, and then slowly, I start exhaling deeply, letting it go with my breathing patterns. The fear inside my chest diminishes and I notice a sense of space inside. It's fleetingly brief, but hey, it's a start. The fear comes crashing back within seconds, but once again, I take note of it, let it crush on my chest, and then breathe it away. I realize that this method is working one moment at a time, and that's huge!

I throw in some free form style, meaning, I add hand motions. I scoop out the fear with my hands and then shake that fear off. I scoop and shake. Scoop and shake. It works. I'm kind of amazed. It's so stupidly simple, yet marvelously effective. The breathe, scoop and shake method lets me know that I can manage this panic. I *will* survive. I *will* be okay. There are times when I "scoop and shake" my way through entire nights.

Next time you feel panic in your soul, try it. Scoop it out and shake it away. Know that you are probably not the only human scooping and releasing right at that moment—I'm with you all the way.

Of course, I want to teach this to the teens at the shelter, but somehow, I can't find a way to explain it succinctly; a way that doesn't make me sound like a total loon. Not only that, but I still don't trust myself. Who am I to hand out advice? I'm walking a thin line. I mean, recently when a resident was caught sneaking alcohol into the shelter in little baggies positioned in her bra, yours truly contemplated drinking her confiscated booze. I've even caught myself eyeing the Xanax medications that some of our residents are on. Let me scoop and shake that away.

In another self-help book, I come across an exercise that seems doable. The exercise is called "Flip Switch" and it's meant to decrease your negative self-talk, while encouraging you to focus on the good things about yourself. You achieve this by appreciating a different thing about yourself every day.

Sure, I'll try it. Every day, for the next 30 days, I'll appreciate something about moi.

Here are some of the things I write over the first few days:

I appreciate that I'm trying this "flipswitch" exercise
I appreciate my skin holding me together
I appreciate that I want to understand
I appreciate that I'm a human being

This flip-switch exercise makes me realize how hard it is for me to find something positive to say about myself. I quit after 11 days.

Roy's first reviews hit the papers. They are not favorable. Rotten Tomatoes gives the film a 37% rotten score and that pleases me. Rotten Tomatoes reports Roy's movie as "borrowing cliché after cliché from other (and better) military branch movies."
Good. No, wait. Excellent. Let Roy eat some humble pie for a change. Let him choke on it. This is a refreshing moment for me, and no, I'm not at my most noble…but on the plus side, I am feeling positive.

I appreciate that Roy's movie is tanking.

My progress is slow. I'm still unbearably lonely and Samantha still deems me lamer than a bad "Power Rangers" episode, but at least I am now fully committed to healing myself. Mission "Heal Niki" is on.

I'm making some headway on my "Things to do" list. I'm less stressed financially; I'm running; I'm doing yoga; I'm journaling; I'm reading; I'm eating less sugar. Now it's time to take a giant leap forward to accomplish one of the steps I've been avoiding—attend an AA meeting.

No more getting blitzed out of my bracket. This time I mean it.

Ah oui, mes amis. I'm a little skeptical myself.

CHAPTER 30

Down and Out on the Town

My first AA meeting is in Newport Beach.

"Hi, I'm Niki. I'm an alcoholic."

I'm extremely uncomfortable. My hands are sweaty, my face is red and my voice sounds too thin. I feel hypocritical identifying as an alcoholic, like I'm trying to cheat my way into this group, sneaking in pretending I'm one of them. Will they know I'm an imposter? I don't really believe I'm an alcoholic. Heavy drinker—yes. Party animal—yes. Blackout periods—yes. But I don't wake up and drink. I don't drink during the day. I don't drink alone. I've never missed work because of being drunk (well, possibly a handful of times). I haven't hurt anyone except myself (oh right, and feasibly Samantha). Am I in denial? Am I an alcoholic?

The AA group certainly doesn't judge me. They don't seem to judge anyone. I'm furiously judging all of them though. Like the bearded, tattooed, rough-tough dude who pipes up: "Back in 1995 when I killed a man..."

Uh, excuse me? I think I'm in the wrong meeting. I'm a lush, not a murderer.

"I hit him with my semi," the man continues. "Didn't even see him...felt the thump, thump as I rode over him. Still haunts me to this day...that sound, that sensation."

Others share their tales. Heart breaking, mind-blowing stories. These alcoholics are frickin hard core. It's an eye-opener for me. Wow, alcohol sure fucks up people's lives. Fucks them up good and proper.

If anything, AA helps me feel better about my own misadventures. At least I haven't robbed a bank, or crashed my car, or lost my family, or physically abused my child, or vomited in my boss's lap. But you can bet your best coin that I never mention my blacking out and coming to in cars, or bedrooms, with strange men on top of me, or how I've driven home with no memory of ever being in my car. I'm not innocent, that's for certain.

I stick to my sobriety. It's not easy. I feel outside of myself and am not a happy camper. There's an undercurrent of intense anxiety cursing through my veins that I can no longer drink quiet. I prickle with so much damn discontent, I feel I might explode; possibly implode. Samantha asks me to watch TV with her, but I can't sit still.

"Maybe tomorrow night" I tell her. "Tonight Shirley's asked me to go out with her."

I'm lying to my daughter. Shirley hasn't asked me, quite the opposite. I've asked Shirley to go out with me. I need to blow off steam and Shirley is my first choice as accomplice steam-blower.

Don't you worry, I'm not going to drink anything other than O'douls. If I drink about six of those I can get a slight buzz on. I'll also bloat up, burp a lot, absorb 400 empty calories, and pee frequently. It's not ideal.

Because Shirley's as discontent as I am, she readily agrees to go out. She scoops me up in her Honda and we shimmy over to Josh Slocum's, a scene-bar right on the harbor front in Newport Beach owned by Dennis Rodman. It's such a meat market, it's sickening. Oh Newport Beach, what a phony-baloney crowd you attract. Yeah, yeah, and here I am, getting my O'doul's buzz on.

Huge candles burn in every corner, which, upon investigation I discover cost $500 a pop. No wonder the drinks here are radically overpriced. They're literally burning thousands of dollars a night in wax.

Wax on—wax off. (No, I've no clue why I wrote that either.)

A few O'douls in, I'm bored, belching, and frustrated. Suddenly I want nothing more than to go home. Shirley, however, is in full party mode with a small cluster of admirers circling her. She slams back drink after drink and I feel a tinge of envy. In the other hand, I'm also happy that I won't be waking up in a strange car/bed/parking lot with a fierce hangover and bruises, or sperm running out of me; riddled with guilt, shame, and self-loathing. No thank you.

I switch to water. Enough with the bloating, baby beer. As the place winds down, I manage to drag Shirley out to the car park and am thankful that she is finally ready to leave. Alas, she suddenly spots a homeless, African man who sits in a wheelchair begging for change. Shirley is a big softie, especially for African people. Maybe it's "white man's guilt" for growing up in South Africa.

She digs in her purse and hands him $20. "I love you," she says drunkenly to him.

His face lights up as he kisses her hand.

"Thank you, beautiful," he says. "You're an angel."

With those huge blue eyes of her, Shirley *is* angelic looking; no matter that her big blue eyes are slippery with inebriation.

"Niki," Shirley tugs on my arm. "Can we take him home? Please?"

Well, no. I can't very well bring a disabled guy into the 500 square foot studio I share with my young daughter. And I highly doubt that Shirley's husband is going to enjoy her arriving home with a homeless, black man in a wheelchair.

Shirley's eyes fill with tears. "I want to let you come home with me," she tells the man.

He starts crying, too. "Thank you, Angel," he says and clings to her hand.

Goddammit. Now I have to be the bad guy and explain that Shirley is not in her right mind. I try to pry his hand off Shirley's, but he holds steady.

"Look, she's drunk," I explain to him. "She can't take you home. First off, we can't fit your chair in our car."

"It collapses" he assures me, and quickly shifts to begin disassembling his chair.

"No, no. She can't take you home," I persist and notice a police car sideling towards us. "She has a husband at home who will freak out."

I turn to Shirley. "Ok, the police are watching us now, so, please get in the car and let me drive." I know that even with four Odoul's in me, I'm legal to drive.

"No, I'm driving. I don't trust anyone else to drive my car." Shirley pushes me away and turns back to the guy. "Help me get your wheelchair in the trunk."

Jesus H&M Christ. It's trickier dealing with Shirley than all the teens at the shelter put together. Drunk people are so annoying. How strange, I've never noticed this before.

Thankfully, a good-looking guy (who had his eye on Shirley earlier) ambles over. I explain to Good-looking that Shirley, in her drunken state, has had this nifty idea to take the disabled vagrant home with her. Plus, the police are now watching us, so I need Shirley to get in the car, and she needs to let me drive.

The guy nods. He understands how this situation could end badly. He hands the homeless man another $20 bill and tells him to vanish. "You won't be getting in this car with these ladies tonight, you got that?" His voice promises a follow through to make good on the semi-threat, and the wheelchair man knows enough to vamoose.

Shirley bursts into tears and sobs onto the man's chest. I wonder if I should call a cab? I desperately want to be at home, but I can't leave my drunk friend with this stranger, even if he is hot and has just saved the day/night.

"You're seriously crazy, Shirley." I tell her. "Please can we go home?"

Shirley smiles at me through her tears.

"I love you, Niki. I wish I was married to you."

She's beautiful, fragile looking. I can see why men melt for her, although right now, I'm more like: I'll show you melting if you don't get your ass in the car.

Thankfully, Shirley climbs into the passenger seat and passes out almost instantly. I take it this means she is ready to leave. Bye sad homeless man, bye slightly aggressive but good-looking stranger, bye watchful policemen, bye disgusting meat-market.

I drive Shirley home where her husband comes out to help me maneuver her inside.

"She loves you so much," I tell him, and have no idea why I feel obliged to lie to the man.

Back in our minuscule home, Samantha watches TV by herself—yes, in the walk-in closet.

"Guess what, mom?" she pipes up the moment I come through the front door. "Did you know that Dolphins sleep with one eye open?" Her face practically radiates with the marvel of learning. "Only the one half of their brain is awake while the other half rests. It's called unihemispheric. If they close their left eye, the right half of the brain goes to sleep. The awake side of the brain guards against danger…oh, and they sleep for 4 hours out of every 24. Isn't that cool."

I did *not* know any of this fantastically, glorious information. I regard my child in wonder and feel enormously lucky. How did I acquire such a perfect daughter? I'm filled with gratitude and feel such love pour out of me towards her it's virtually palpable. I want to throw my arms about her and weep with thankfulness.

"Would you like some tea?" I ask instead.

She nods, and I prepare a little pot of rooibos tea.

"I love you, Samantha." I tell her as I go to sit alongside her in the closet. I nestle into the floor pillows, sip my tea, pat Samantha's thigh, and realize I am 100 % completely content.

CHAPTER 31

Lack

My contentment doesn't last long even though I wish it would. How do I get contentment to be my baseline? I'm hell bent on changing my negative thoughts into positive ones. I'm going to think myself happy. I've already ascertained that 90% of my thoughts are negative, a constant stream of: no one will ever love me; I'm a loser; I'm getting old; I'll never have enough money; I'll never make it as a musician; I'll never have papers, or be able to travel; Roy didn't love me; Dean didn't love me; my mother didn't love me—which brings me hurtling back to "no one will ever love me." Then all those negative thoughts lead to this one: Oh God, I'm making my body sick. I'm probably riddled with cancer by now from all this toxic unhappiness coagulating inside me.

Well hell. Who can be content with that shit going on 24/7?

I acknowledge what my mind has been up to and it's not very comely. Paying attention to my negative self-talk, I notice the barrage of unhelpful thoughts that I aim, not only at myself, but also at innocent people, pretty much all day long. I've a shit ton of work to do, but at least I'm aware of it now. I vow to change my thinking. The next time I catch myself dumping negativity all over myself, I say out loud: "Hey, Niki. You are not a loser."

Hearing me protest myself makes me laugh out loud, and again I realize, this might just work.

Not only do I want to improve myself, I want to improve my parenting abilities as well. Being more aware of my thoughts and behaviors brings me to realize how I act at times towards my daughter. I admit to Samantha: "I know I sometimes react if you take long showers, or eat all the leftovers in the fridge—I can't help it. It's a kneejerk reaction, but honestly, I want you to know that you are welcome to eat any food at any time, and take showers as often as you want. Just ignore my ridiculous reactions."

Samantha doesn't bat an eye. "That's okay, mom. I know you have scarcity thinking."

I don't even rightfully know what scarcity thinking is and have to research it immediately. Slam-dunk for Samantha because she is 100% correct. My mind is rife with "scarcity thinking." I've struggled to make ends meet for most of my life, so sure, scarcity thinking is understandable. But now that it has been brought to my attention, I realize that my continuous viewpoint of "will I get through the month" has overlapped into other areas of my life. To be more accurate, it has permeated every single aspect of my world. By this I mean I never buy myself anything. My clothes come mainly from the shelter's donation closet, or are other people's hand me downs. When I go out to dinner, I order the cheapest thing on the menu, even if it isn't really something I want, and even when I'm *not* the one paying the bill. My car is run down, unwashed and unloved. So is my body. I haven't had a physical checkup in years. I've never had a manicure, or a facial, or a massage. Those seem like a luxury exclusively meant for, well… other people.

My thinking is all about "cheap". I buy the cheapest food, clothes, shampoos, furniture…you name it. This means I skimp on my health, my looks, my life; and that Samantha has had to make do with some woefully sub-par Christmas and birthday presents.

My scarcity mindset shows my lack of trust/belief in the universe. It screams that I will not be provided for—that God (or whichever higher power you subscribe to) doesn't love me quite as much as he loves the others. That I will always be alone. That I will always be struggling. That I don't deserve to be happy. That I don't deserve a decent man. That I am less than. Naturally, I treat myself accordingly, and am not surprised when others treat me that way, too. For me it's all lack, lack, lackity-lack. I absolutely view the world through my self-imposed poverty lenses—poor me.

All at once I understand the passage in the bible where it says: The rich get richer and the poor get poorer. Quite simply it correlates to if you are happy with who you are and at peace with your life, then everything takes on a shine. You can't help but notice beauty and kindness in the world wherever you look. But if you're despondent and hate your life (like I have done for the past two years) then you are probably more prone to focus on the shitty stuff going on. The saying refers to "being rich in spirit" not "being rich in coinage" as I'd always thought.

Part of this "rich in spirit" stuff comes from being generous, which is problematic for me because, that's right, I have scarcity thinking. I am not a giver. Shit no. I'm definitely a taker. I constantly survey my environment for what it can provide me. What can he/she/they/you give me? To be completely honest, sometimes I take without asking. Yes, I believe it is called stealing. I rationalize that my poverty entitles me to help myself—like clothes from the shelter for example, or toilet paper from swanky restaurants. Roy certainly doesn't know that I've continuously stuffed toilet rolls in my handbag whenever he took me out for a meal.

Since I want, yet don't seem to receive, I've been stuck in a mammoth pity party, constantly wondering: hey, when's my turn coming? When am I gonna get mine? And who the hell's gonna give it to me? Umm, paging Roy—come in please.

To make it worse, even when I *do* get—where the heck is my gratitude? Okay sure, I'm poor, but there are millions who are poorer. Yes, I'm getting old, but there are millions who don't get the privilege of aging. So what if I live in a tiny apartment? There are millions who are homeless. Who cares that I'm not married? I have a wonderful daughter, and there are millions who never get to experience the joy of parenthood. All things considered, I'm amazingly lucky.

This new clarity illuminates for me that I haven't been focused on living my life. I've been avoiding my life, and feverishly hoping to live Roy's life. I'm pretty sure he felt it too—me smothering him in my desperate energy. No wonder he wanted out. Why on earth should Roy marry me, pay for me, look after me, feed me, stimulate and entertain me? What does he get in return? A whole lot of flimflam, that's what.

I switch out my victim thinking of "how can Roy/God/the universe do this to me?" to a healthier perspective of "thank you Roy/God/the Universe for bringing me these challenges to allow me to grow."

What radical shift is this in my thinking? And why am I spouting out psychobabble like I've hit the mother-load of self-actualization?

I don't know, but the profound adjustment of "it's not happening **to** you—it's happening **for** you" makes me want to stop asking what the world can do for me, and ask instead, what can I do for this world?

Suddenly I feel enormous amounts of love for everybody and I honestly want to make their lives better in whatever way I can. What are these very un-like me thoughts of "how can I be of service to others?"

A warm glow flows through me and I'm excited to go out and love all over my fellow humans. Watch out, good people.

CHAPTER 32

Yo-yo, yoga

Isn't it funny how when you finally let go (kicking and screaming) of your negative nonsense, something positive pops right up?

"Niki, how would you like to teach the kids here yoga?" Colleen asks me one day at work.

Yes, please. I would like it. I would like it very much. What a wonderful way to spread my newfound goodwill.

Colleen signs me up for a weekend course designed specifically to learn how to teach yoga to teenagers. I enjoy all 20 hours of the course, and soon after, show up at the shelter dressed in comfy pants with my yoga mat in hand—ready to change the world from my spongy, foam bedrock.

Teaching yoga to the teens proves to be immensely rewarding. At first, I'm super nervous. What if I injure a kid? What if I forget the routine I'm teaching? What if they don't listen? What if they loathe doing yoga?

Thing is, the kids often do loathe yoga, and they absolutely let me know about it.

"Why do we have to do this? It's so lame."

Slowly I learn how to work around the stumbling blocks. For those teens that think yoga is "lame", I perform the 8-*angle Pose*. It is impressive looking although not really that hard to do.

The teens immediately want to learn how to do it, and suddenly yoga becomes "cool". For boys who think yoga is only for girls and sissys, I teach them *Crow Pose*—where you balance all your weight on your hands. I take it a step further and shoot back into *Plank Pose*. It takes a significant amount of arm and abdominal strength to conquer this maneuver, and the boys welcome the chance to show off their man-strength in front of the girls. A lot of the boys can do some rather amazing things with their bodies once they understand the techniques. Not to be sexist, because of course the girls can too, although girls tend to excel in flexibility rather than sheer strength. They have spines that bend every which way. Oh, the joy of being young.

If there are overweight kids in the class who are self-conscious of their bodies, I incorporate plenty of relaxation poses and am mindful to stick with easy poses that won't "show them up".

I learn to deal with farting: real farting and pretend farting sounds (that prove to be rather popular during class). If a teen lets one slip out and is embarrassed, I explain that this is a completely natural phenomenon, and actually healthy. In fact, there is a position called *Wind Relieving Pose* that is almost guaranteed to make you push out some air. The kids find this hilarious.

I discover that children who have been sexually abused do not like poses that call for them to spread their legs wide apart. A pose like *Warrior Two* makes them feel too exposed; too vulnerable. For girls that have been raped, *Warrior Two* is difficult. Funny thing is that *Warrior Two* is the exact pose that helps build up self-esteem and trust in your own body. It's known as *Proud Warrior*.

Regrettably, we encounter a lot of rape victims at the shelter. Girls that have been raped by their relatives: fathers, brothers, uncles and cousins. Girls that have been raped by mom's new boyfriend and mom won't believe them (usually because she doesn't want to lose said boyfriend). Girls that have been raped by peers or teachers. Girls that have been raped by strangers—as is the case with our latest resident, a striking 16-year-old named Carly. We get to learn more about her at staff meeting as Carly reads her "This is Me" paper aloud to us.

"I'm Carly. I live with my mom and younger brother in Oceanside."

Carly has that sun-kissed look: blonde hair, perfect skin, blue eyes. She's stunning.

"I came to the shelter because…" Carly hesitates. "I don't want to talk about the reasons why I'm here."

"That's okay," Colleen assures her. "You don't have to say anything you're not comfortable with."

Carly continues, "I'm most proud of myself for getting good grades at school."

Carly does get excellent grades at school, which is uncommon for our demographic. The teens we see at the shelter usually aren't focused on schoolwork. Concentrating on schoolwork can seem rather futile if your father is beating or raping you, or your mother's getting high all the time—right?

"When I leave the shelter I hope to be able to go back to my old life like it was before." Carly's voice trails off as she smiles limply.

Carly's therapist fills us in on her case. Carly went to a party, drank way too much, and blacked out. While she was unconscious, six guys raped her and filmed themselves doing it, like they were being awesome or something. Carly doesn't remember a thing—she was out cold.

With an upcoming court date and her case in the newspapers, Carly is understandably mortified—but none of this is why Carly is at our shelter. The reason that Carly is in our shelter is that her mother blames her for the rape. The mom asserts that Carly "asked" for it by the way she behaves, the way she dresses, the way she drinks too much. Imagine going through something as scary and humiliating as being raped by six guys, and then have your mother be unsupportive? Already teeming with self-recrimination, Carly says she can't handle being at home right now. It's too painful for her.

I feel for Carly. How would I react if Samantha had been raped by six guys? I'd be insanely outraged. I'd want to kill those guys. Most certainly I would never in a trillion years think that it was Samantha's fault. That thought wouldn't even enter my head, however, if it were me that was raped by six guys during one of my blackouts, I'd absolutely think that it *was* my fault. Dammit, clearly I have more self-work to do.

I recognize Carly's mom the moment she flounces in through the front door of the shelter. She couldn't be anyone else's mother with her blue-eyes, blonde hair and long legs—they are a handsome family.

"Hi sweetie," she smiles at Carly who doesn't smile back but instead gapes at her mother with a look of disbelief on her face.

"Are those my jeans you're wearing?" Carly asks incredulously.

The mom doesn't miss a beat, "Yeah, they look fab on me, don't they?"

This brief interaction explains their entire relationship to me.

I completely understand why Carly is unwilling to do *Warrior Two* pose. It's something we'll have to build up to over the next few weeks. Yoga is about connecting with your body, and if your body has been through trauma, sometimes that connection is scary to re-establish.

At the end of each class I have the teens lie down on their yoga mats in *Shavasana* (corpse pose) and tell them that I'll be coming around the room to "adjust" them, and that they can raise their hand if they don't want me to touch them. A young boy raises his hand and voices that he is uncomfortable with this "adjustment". I know this small child has been physically abused, so I appreciate him setting and protecting his boundaries.

"No problem," I tell him.

The "adjustment" that I administer is this: I massage the top of their heads, I press their shoulders towards the floor and I rub their feet. It's wonderful to see and feel the teens visibly relax under my touch. These poor kids don't get to experience a lot of nurturing touch. The bulk of their human touch is either violent or sexual in nature. I feel privileged to be able to give them a loving touch that has no negative or threatening undertones.

Most children enjoy the "adjustment" but I discover that autistic children do not. For them, having their heads massaged is actually painful. Physical touch is too much for them. It's not just touch that upsets them. It can be light, sound and smells too. An autistic brain struggles to filter out excess stimuli leaving the child overwhelmed by sensory input.

Following about five classes, the young boy who doesn't want me to "adjust" him suddenly pipes up: "Miss Niki, today can you do that thing that you do to the others at the end of class?"

Absolutely I can, and it warms my heart that I've earned his trust. Another thing I do while the teens lie in *Shavasana* is I have them take a moment to acknowledge their bodies.

"Send your body some appreciation," I encourage them. "I know it's easy to criticize the body. It's easy to think: I'm too fat, too short, too thin, too knock-kneed whatever—so just for a moment, send your body a positive message. Realize what a fabulous piece of machinery your body is and how hard it works for you on a daily basis. Know that this body you inhabit is the vehicle that you have for this lifetime. So be good to it. Send it some love."

During *Shavasana*, I notice that Carly has tears running down her cheeks. I take it as a sign that she is opening up, and that is gratifying to me. She's taking steps towards healing. You'd be amazed how many people cry during *Shavasana*. I, myself, shed tears at the end of every single class when I first started practicing yoga. It's the body accessing and releasing trapped emotions—marvelous stuff. I'm hopeful that Carly is reconnecting to her body and liberating some of the horror trapped in there.

I spend extra time with Carly during yoga class, teaching her all kinds of poses to empower her, and at the end of her stay during her final yoga class, Carly stands proud and firm in a beautiful rendition of *Warrior Two*. It brings tears to my eyes. Go Carly, go. Is there any bigger reward in the world?

Within a few months of teaching yoga, I have it down. I know which kids are forming trysts and will consequently be problematic standing next to each other. I separate them before class even starts. I know to make the girls change their low-cut tops, or the boys will not be able to concentrate. All yoga clothing is suitable, long hair is tied up, bangs are pinned back, mats are clean, the music is soothing, and hey presto—ladies and gentlemen, we have a yoga class for teenagers.

Teaching yoga consistently helps me, too. I leave the class with a sense of peace and gratitude. There is one time, however, that I smack a young lady in the face—how very un-yoga-ly of me. It's during *Shavasana* and all the teens are lying still while I perform my "nurturing" touch on them. I'm bent down working on one of the kids, when suddenly the girl alongside me lets out an obnoxious scream.

She's been making these squawking, orally expulsive sounds all day. I know it's not that she's in pain or anything like that, she's doing it for attention. Before I can check myself, I slap the back of my hand against her face, and hiss out a "shhhhh".

I don't know who is more surprised, me or her. I'm horrified at myself. Where the hell did my serenity go? How can I physically lash out at one of the residents? I've never done anything like that in all my years of working at the shelter. Her yell was so invasive that I simply had a knee jerk reaction to it.

Luckily for me, this young lass believes that my slap is part of her adjustment. In fact, she thanks me for slapping her and lets me know how it helped to calm her. Well, there's a relief, and mercifully, I have not hit any of my yoga students since—mind you, no on has screamed in my ear since either, so...

For the most part, the teens enjoy yoga and frequently come to thank me afterwards. I find a little note in my staff office box that says "Thank you for coming to teach us every week. We love doing yoga and we love you—Megan" (this is her real name in case she ever reads this).

I have a young boy tell me that while he was on an outing with his parents, things started going badly. He relates how an argument flared up, but then he heard my voice in his head, saying, "Breathe in, breathe out." This reminded him to focus on his breathing and relax into his body, and he stopped arguing. Oh my God, that young boy made me feel like a goddam million dollars.

Thank you, Colleen for giving me the opportunity to be of service by doing something I love. I'm beyond happy to supply these young people with a coping skill that is loving and healthy. I know they need all the help they can get. I know I need all the help I can get, therefore I teach yoga at as many places that will have me. I want to teach in schools, offices, at conferences, in prisons. I want to take yoga to the streets and teach everyone for free. I want my fellow beings to experience the joy that this mind/body/spirit connection brings. Seriously. Look me up, I'll teach you.

CHAPTER 33

Two Weeks of Bizarreness

My heartache is changing. Moving. Subsiding. Thank you, body chemistry for finally easing up on me. I wonder what Elizabeth Kübler-Ross would have thought of my clumsy muddling through her model of the stages of grief? I believe I did the denial and bargaining part in the beginning. I even did that begging part on my knees (oh good, you remember). I lingered in depression like a pregnant elephant—far too long an ordeal, and then smashed my way through the angry part. I've done all the phases, just not in quite the right order.

There's one left—acceptance. Bring it. Halle-frickin-lujah. Let's get me some succor sucker.

I'm not the only one making progress. My steady workmate, Ben, is moving forward in his life, too. He is nearing completion on earning his Master's Degree (and I couldn't be prouder of him). For the past three years, Ben has not only worked full time, but has studied full time, too. That's Ben: super mensch.

He asks me one day if I'd mind being a Guinea pig for his final project. He needs a "pretend" patient to film a therapy session with for his professor. Would I mind if he films me having a therapy session with him? Not at all, my very lovely friend, Ben, I'm flattered. And since I now believe that I have my shit solidly together, I fully expect to "pilot" this therapy session to make Ben look magnificently professional. Oh, the presumption. Oh, the ego.

Ben hits record on the camera and starts asking me questions to establish a time-line of my life. He probes deeper to find out what the big moments were in my childhood, my young adulthood, as a parent for Samantha, and so on. I answer as honestly as possible, because I seriously do want this to be beneficial for Ben (and for me). All is going smoothly, until Ben revisits an event that I mentioned happened when I was 15.

"Can you tell me more about that event?" he asks innocently.
I want to tell Ben about this experience, I really do, but somehow the words won't come out my mouth.

"Sorry Ben, but I don't think I want to talk about that, actually," I say, suddenly conscious of the camera recording this session.

"Not a problem," he says. "We can move on."

Ben continues his questioning, but now my hearing seems to be to fading out. Not only can I not hear Ben properly (although he is right next to me), I can't fully understand his questions anymore. It's like I'm suddenly listening and thinking through a thick brain fog. I shake my head at Ben in confusion.

"I'm struggling to hear you…and understand you." I say, and notice I'm scratching hard at my arms, though I'm not sure what I'm scratching at.

Because Ben is a blossoming therapist of rare quality, he smiles kindly at me and says: "That's okay, Niki, you're disassociating, that's all. It's a way for you to escape having to feel your feelings."

Huh? Well, I'll be a monkey's uncle. Good people, this is not my first therapy session. I know all about disassociation, which is what makes this all the more illuminating for me. Am I not the one who has been on a quest to connect to myself on a deeper level? Do I not urge my yoga students to feel their bodies; to get in touch with themselves? Have I not read volumes on emotional intelligence, and journal-ed myself into supposed clarity? Indeed, I have. Yet here I am steering clear of my own feelings, and only now realize that I've been doing so for many, many years.

The session ends with me in a bit of a daze. My mind is boggling, recalling all the times this fog has pervaded my head, and how I've always dismissed it as I'm hungry, or I have low blood pressure. I think back to arguments I had with Roy, where I stopped arguing mid-sentence because I'd lost my train of thought. Interesting. (Interesting for me that is—it may not be that noteworthy for you).

Ben's "fake" session shakes me up. I am determined to experience my feelings. This time I won't back away. I won't disassociate. I won't panic. I'll stand firm and go through my goddamn feelings, even if it kills me. Ergo—two weeks of bizarreness.

It's not something I can rationally explain. It begins with the sense that an enormous chasm is opening right below, but dangerously close to, my conscious level. It's acutely unsettling. Subconsciously, I grasp this chasm is about to spew forth major unpleasantness, which makes my mind slap into some kind of clumsy overdrive. I'm thinking a mile a minute, bouncing and flouncing all over the show, unwittingly trying to block the oncoming storm.

But you can't outthink a storm, and the first blast hits as I'm walking home from a coffee shop. I know the tsunami has arrived and break into a run because I hate crying in front of other people and my neighbors are lurking all over the show. I slam through my front door, collapse into the nearest chair, and howl like a wounded animal. It's a meltdown par excellence. I sob with such gusto; my lungs could be in jeopardy of disintegrating.

At first, it's a purely physical act, an outpouring of unmitigated grief. Sorrow after sorrow. Wound upon wound. Disappointment after disappointment. I wail out years of hurt and unfathomable grief. After a while, I try to figure out what I'm most sad about, what triggered this? I can't discern anything in particular, there isn't one thought attached to my grief, there isn't much thought at all actually, it's just that my body simply won't stop crying. Then, inexplicably, I start laughing. Now, I'm laughing and crying at the same time, but for the life of me, I can't figure out what the hell is going on. Somehow I've swung from major grief to extreme elation—still, I can't stop crying. It's like my body simply needs to purge this excess emotion.

Hey Ben, I think I'm feeling!

A fly catches my eye as it lands on a table nearby and I stare at it in awe. Wow! This fly is completely beautiful—profoundly, deeply beautiful. I sweep my hand lovingly towards the fly but stop short, stunned by the sight of my own hand. It's as if I'm seeing my hand for the first time in my life, because like the fly, my hand is suddenly perfect. PERFECT. Incredible. Amazing. I'm filled with such wonder that my chest aches. Tears stream as I wrap my arms around myself and basically start speaking in tongues…well, English tongues. It is that the words are foreign to me because I have not said them before.

"I love you so much, Niki." I say, hugging myself tight. "So incredibly much."

And I mean it with every fiber of my being. I kiss my shoulders, my arms, my hands, whatever I can reach. I'm overcome with emotion as I say over and over: "I'm so proud of you, Niki. So, incredibly proud."

Holy Eureka. Dear readers, I believe I've reconnected to a part deep within me that has been cut off for many years. It feels like a homecoming, and I've missed me so very much. I've longed for me. Pined for me. Now, I'm bursting with utter love and admiration for myself. Behold this incredible love—masses and masses of it—pouring into me and out of me.

Welcome home, Niki Smart.

This euphoric high lasts for two days. Everyone and everything I encounter is absolutely flawless. I teeter between smiling so hard that my face hurts to weeping waterworks of joy. I'm nothing but emotion. I feel ridiculously lucky just to be alive. How fantastic is this? It's glorious—way better than being drunk.

Regrettably, after two days it all comes crashing down. Now I find myself horribly irritated with everyone and everything. Nothing seems right and all humans suck. How did I swing from "I love everyone" to "get the fuck away from me"? This sheer irritation lasts the whole day. It's a discontent akin to steel wool scratching on sensitive skin. I'm raw with annoyance, unable to find a comfortable way to exist, and no matter how I try I can't regain my bliss from the day before.

That night, I dream that Samantha is 5 years old again and upset about something. Although I'm standing right next to her, she crawls onto my mother's lap for comfort and I'm so jealous I could explode. Next thing, Samantha has morphed into an adult, and I'm trying to drown her. She does not resist me. She is allowing me to drown her. I stop, and tell her I can't do it. I can't drown her. I wake up crazy crying, searing with jealousy, anger, and regret—such regret it takes my breath away. I can't understand my dreams, or what is happening to me.

I phone Ben, who assures me that this is simply me feeling my feelings, and that because I've opened this doorway, everything is magnified right now. Of course, Ben is right.

My feelings aren't done expelling. The worst emotion that begs to be dealt with arises slowly. An uncomfortable nagging to remember something, but I can't quite grasp the memory. It's something ugly that I haven't looked at properly. Something that still needs to surface.

And surface it does. At 2 a.m. in the morning. Suddenly, I'm wide-awake—on full alert. I don't know what has woken me, but slicing into my mind are visions of my grandfather molesting me at age nine. I see his face, feel his hands on me, and I feel sick, sick, sick. Sick to my stomach.

As sexual abuse survivor, Elizabeth Smart said: "I remember exactly how I felt after he raped me. How broken I felt. That I was beyond all help, all hope—that even if someone did find me, what was the point? I was useless. I was disgusting. I wasn't worth saving at that point. I thought of the other children who I'd seen on the news and how their stories always seemed to end so tragically, and I couldn't help but think, they are the lucky ones." [1]

Thoughts of my prolonged molestation parlay into the many one night stands I've had—one night stands that came about because I'd learned to perpetuate the initial abuse upon myself. I think of one

---

[1] From "My Story" by Elizabeth Smart on TEDx University of Nevada

undesirable man after another that has stuck his penis in me. I want to throw up. Revulsion judders through my very core. My face grinds in pure disgust. I'm filled with nausea. How could I have let all those guys do that to me? Urrgh!
Shame—the deepest, darkest of emotions. No fun to deal with at all.

The next day I have zero motivation. I manage to make breakfast but it proves pointless. I have no appetite. Nothing sounds good. Not food, not anything. I decide to get back into bed, and if I need to cry and sleep the whole day, so be it. I'm taking a mental health day. I need to, because I'm exhausted and feebly fragile, and my instinct is to nurture myself to the best of my ability. I don't make any plans. I don't want to go out. I want to stay home and get through this thing—whatever this thing is.

At this point, I've been crying on and off for about 2 weeks, but during my "mental health sick day" an awareness arises that the *way* I'm crying is physiologically different to how I usually cry.

Here's the difference:

1. I don't get snotty, there's not much mucus involved here. It's essentially only tears.
2. A peculiar, low whoosh sound comes out my mouth the whole time I cry, as if a muted wind is being pushed from my lungs. It is not a noise I recognize from any previous crying sessions (and we know I've had a few).
3. I don't feel sorry for myself at all. There is no self-pity here. What I *do* feel is extremely protective of myself.
4. I have a strong sense that this emotional storm is very necessary. That I need to release this, whatever this is.

I come to the realization that this is not *reactive* crying to someone or something that has hurt me. This is a cry of acknowledgement. Deep acknowledgement. This is my very being saying: I hear you, Niki, and I *feel* your pain.

Holy shit, Ben! I want to kiss you right now. Thank you for helping me open up my blocked being. Thank you for helping me to recognize and restore myself.

You're a goddamn bona fide wizard.

CHAPTER 34

Revisiting the Blood Sucking Monster

Having run the gamut of emotions from euphoric high to deep revulsion, my two weeks of physically/mentally/emotionally purgative bizarreness subside, and I stabilize. I'm back to normal, but I want more than normal. I want that awe-inspiring "high on life" feeling to come back. How can I get that feeling on a daily basis? Can I? Can anyone? Hello?

This business of feeling connected to myself brings with it a new awareness. I start to see the multitude of things I've done because I haven't valued myself. The way I've gone back to Roy over and over. Well shit damn, no more of that. Or the many times I've gone out and endured dates and sex that I wasn't really interested in just to please the other person. Why did I do that? No self-worth, that's why. And how did I cope? I drank.

Sure, I'll go on a date with someone, even if they're a bit of a troll, as long as I can drink masses and get nicely numbed up. And then, if Mr. Troll wants to have sex? No problem—but can you please first point me towards the Jägermeister?

Now that I value myself, I'm not prepared to do anything that may harm me—and I don't care how much alcohol someone has available. I don't really even want to drink anymore. It seems pointless now. I won't be present for the moment; the alcohol will damage my body; the hangover will ruin my day. All those hangovers—all that poison—my poor liver—my poor body. This is wild. It's such a new concept feeling this self-value and self-worth. It's going to take some getting used to.

Since I've not been that kind to myself before, I read all about loving-kindness. Turns out that if you learn to operate from this gentle outlook, it will elevate your life. Who doesn't want that? I know I do. I vow to be not only kinder to myself, but also to my fellow humans (lucky yous).

At the shelter, I'm dealing with Chad, a young man who is a fulltime job just by himself. His attention-seeking behavior is through the roof. He's sneaky and insolent, but also hilarious and charming. He coerces his roommate into swallowing one end of a long piece of purple yarn, while he swallows the other. They both keep swallowing the string until they're a foot apart, then they shuffle downstairs to come and show staff how they are joined by an umbilical cord. They think it's hysterical (and it *is* pretty funny) until they try to tug the wool back out of their throats. Yeah, not quite as hilarious. Amidst painful retching sounds, they coax yarn out of their esophagi.

Does this experience deter them? Not in the least. Next up, they draw crude genitalia on the dining room table (again, it is pretty funny). It also takes a lot of sandpapering to remove.

Once his roommate exits the shelter, young Chad is by himself. With no one to give him the attention he craves, Chad ramps up his "you *will* notice me" behavior by stuffing his toilet full of tampons. Then he goes number two atop his little feminine hygiene mountain …and flushes. And wouldn't you know it, his toilet is right above the staff office where I'm seated at a computer working on client files.

All at once, an offensive smell permeates the office and brown liquid starts dripping onto my files. Looking up, I see gross sewage goop seeping through the ceiling, and this muck is dousing our client files in foul shit smelling liquid. It is wholly revolting, and the worst of it is that it's *my* duty to mop up this noxious mess.

I know instantly that this is Chad's doing because he is the only client upstairs, plus the empty box of tampons next to his clogged toilet is a bit of a giveaway.

Latex gloves on, I wipe, and scrub, and scoop, trying not to breathe. The whole time, I hate on Chad big time. What a little dipshit. Why would he do this? It's so not fair. Now I have to work way harder, and it's not like I'll get paid more. This is seriously beyond the call of duty. And what if I pick up some bacterial infection? Will Chad pay for my medical fees? No, of course not. Little brat.

Three repulsive hours later, everything is clean, and I hate my job much more than usual. The endless stream of venom swirling non-stop in my mind segues from what a douchebag Chad is, to how my shelter job is debasing, low-paid bullshit. Fuck this job. I'm supposed to be a major pop star for fuck's sake, not swabbing up shit all night long.

I hear Chad coming downstairs and know he's headed to the office door. Part of me is ready to rain a ton of hurt down on this boy. I'm going to give him a razor-sharp piece of my mind. But as I open the door, something in me shifts. Again, I'm not quite sure how this happens—maybe it's the look on his face? Or maybe it is a moment of self-recognition? I'm not sure what, but I literally feel myself soften. Instead of being mad at him, I *see* him. I mean, I *really* see him. Here he stands before me, a young boy struggling to make sense of his life; a life that I know from his file includes witnessing his father repeatedly beating his mother, and this same mother secretly blaming Chad for the beatings. Naturally, Chad is full of self-doubt, and his constant peacocking is simply a way to supply himself some much needed stature and the illusion that he is safe. How can I be mad at him? I can't.

"It's all clean," I tell him. "And I managed to save all the files, no harm done."

Chad clumsily apologizes. "Uh...I'm sorry. I thought it would be funny. I didn't know this...what a mess."

"It's okay, Chad." I say. "Thank you for apologizing. That really helps me."

Score one for loving-kindness. I feel goddamn magnanimous about our interaction.

Hey, look at me, Roy—I'm becoming virtuous.

Things could have gone differently between Chad and myself. I could've told him his behavior was unacceptable and juvenile, and that he would be receiving a consequence for his actions. Chad would then most probably have become defensive, yelled out that I suck, that the shelter sucks, and that he wants to leave. Neither of us would have felt good. Neither of us would have learnt anything. Both of us would have been stuck in our own self-righteous indignation.

Instead, Chad beams at me, grateful that I'm not mad at him—and I beam back, grateful that I'm not mad at him. A connection has been made. Outstanding.

Though this is a minor interaction, I feel like I've hit the jackpot. I've found the missing piece. Here is my proof that operating with an attitude of loving-kindness can elevate my life. And what's more, I realize that it's *my* choice. I can react with anger or love, but I will indeed be lifted to a higher disposition if I approach all beings with loving kindness no matter my frame of mind. In other words, if I'm in a foul mood, that shouldn't give me the right to be rude to someone. If I'm in a hurry, that shouldn't make it okay to dismiss someone. If I feel wronged, that shouldn't give me the right to lash out at someone.

Loving-kindness is a way of existing in the world **at all times**, not just when it's convenient, or when I'm in the humor for it. I get it, and now I'm excited to try it out again—to react with love not antagonism or irritation, or boredom, or irreverence, or sarcasm—only love.

I decide to practice on a staff member that I typically avoid because she has a grating voice. With my new approach, I see how unkind it is of me to avoid and judge her just because of the timbre of her voice. I give it some thought, and the next time I'm on shift with her, I reach out to her.

"Hi Judy, how's it going?"

She's surprised, precisely because I always ignore her.

"Good. Thanks." Oh boy, there's that voice, but—loving-kindness.

"I have some clothes that I hardly wear. Would you have any interest in them?"

Naturally, I've appropriated the bulk of these items from the shelter over the years, but that's not the point here. (Yes, I admit I'm a petty thief, but I'm giving something away that I have in my possession to someone that I don't really enjoy—for me that's a BIG step forward, okay?)

It's ridiculous, but it pleases me no end when Judy accepts the bag of clothes. Watching her smile as she rummages through "my" old clothes makes me feel God like. And no wonder, because God *is* love, and today, good people, so am I. I'm brimming with love.

I think of all the times that I've been dismissive to a client because they didn't seem worth my attention. All the times I've hurled insults at the drivers in front of me. All the times I've ignored people, or cut them short because I wasn't interested in what they were saying—or in a hurry—or too self-involved.

I realize that I thought of the shelter as "a blood-sucking monster that takes, and takes, and takes", and then I lumped Roy into that same category; after all, he was taking *everything* from me—my entire future. But I see now that my love for Roy was not love. It was desperation. That was me trying to get my childhood needs met. That was me hoping that somehow Roy would make my life splendiferous and save me the hassle. That was me operating out of fear, not operating from love. Fear of rejection, and quite possibly fear of connection, as well.

Looking back, I can plainly see that I forced Roy to be my lifeline, and then I hung on for dear life. When Roy broke up with me, I sensed my fantasy future world slipping away from me, and my automatic reaction was to tighten my grip. This clinging intensified my feelings of being powerless and inadequate, and when we feel inadequate or unworthy, we tend to hoard things. I was so afraid of losing anything and everything—from Roy's attention to $1. Of course, clinging and grasping exacerbates scarcity thinking, which leads to more clinging and grasping—and down the lack-of-love rabbit hole we go. How can

I give you love when I'm starving for it myself? And I was starving, mainly because I didn't love myself.

As Pema Chödrön says about loving kindness and compassion in her book "When Things Fall Apart":

> *To the degree that we have compassion for ourselves, we will have compassion for others.*

True that, Pema. You awesome monk, you.

Suddenly, I have a revelation. I have been a big blood-sucking monster myself. Possibly neither the shelter, nor Roy, were taking anything from me? Maybe I was simply incapable of giving?

To any of you that have suffered at the hand of my ignorance, please forgive me.

CHAPTER 35

Peace out

I treat the teens at the shelter with newfound respect. I treat my co-workers with newfound respect. I treat Samantha with newfound respect. I treat myself with newfound respect. Life becomes easier, and I am progressively happier.

One day I realize that I no longer think about Roy. I'm not in love with him anymore. He could bring ten girls over to my small apartment and have sex with them on my kitchen table, I simply wouldn't care.

"Mind you don't get sperm in the fruit bowl," I'd say with aplomb. Don't be silly; of course I don't own a fruit bowl.

Out of the blue, I receive an email from Roy. He tells me that he's getting married—to a young woman. Younger than me by 15 years. Ouch! He says he has reservations though, and signs his missive "still haven't found what I'm looking for."

Part of me wants to yell: "You Mormon moron—I'm right here waiting for you" but another part of me knows that Roy is on a different path to me. Sure, it's easy to preach and point fingers, so that's why I'm going to do it. Hey, I've "labored" comprehensively to discover myself, but Roy is still suffering panic attacks due to his failed career, and is now having a quick "band aid wedding" with a woman half his age to keep the bogeyman at bay. Roy hasn't found what he's looking for because he's still seeking external approval from everywhere and everyone (yes, that does ring a bell). Roy needs to do some soul searching to uncover the things in himself that he doesn't approve of and rectify them so he *is* able to approve of himself. Exactly! Like me realizing that I've been a blood-sucking monster; that I'm cheap; that I'm penny-pinching and ungenerous; that I use alcohol to block out everything which makes me stay stuck, and then I wonder "Hey! Why am I stuck?" That I'm impatient and want everything NOW, dammit. That I'm a taker who struggles to give because I've been shut down and closed off.

Once Roy can view himself more honestly, possibly he can heal his wounds and reconnect to his being? Then he wouldn't need to search anymore. I know: so simple—so terribly complex.

Self-discovery is bloody hard. I mean, it took me several years and ample hoopla to make that painful inner journey, so I won't judge Roy (okay, maybe a bit—okay maybe a big bit).

I'll tell you what I will judge though—I will judge religion. I believe that soaking your children in religious rigmarole is a form of child abuse. Poor Roy has layers and layers of damaging religious beliefs woven tightly around his penis, and they're going to be a bitch to unravel. Listen up Mormon Church! Sex is *not* sinful. Masturbation is not a perversion of the body's passions. Oral sex is not evil. Committing a sexual transgression is not *nearly as bad as murdering someone*. Women *do not* have to be virtuous any more so than men do. And sorry Roy, but showering twice a day *won't* keep you uncontaminated.

Life cannot be placed neatly within a box. Life is a messy, fantastic, terrifying, satisfying, thrilling shit-show extravaganza. I hope that Roy can work through enough layers to enable him to: "find what he *is* looking for". With any luck he can at least find some peace of mind in his new marriage. I want that for him.

More than anything though, I root for Roy to wrap his arms around himself and say, "I love you, Roy" and truly mean it. From there I bet it'll be Oingo Boingo all the way home for him.

Now don't think that because I teach yoga, read oodles of "self-help" books, and have discovered a sort of magic "loving kindness" button, that my life is 100 % peachy. Hell no. There are moments when I loathe my life, but there are many *more* moments when I flat out love my life. That's what it's all about though, isn't it? The ups *and* the downs. We have to have the bad to recognize the good, and vice versa. When I hit a low, I can easily descend into the familiar dark hole, except, now I recognize it as such. I further know that my "dark side" can teach me something if I dig into it. I can approach it with curiosity. I can even befriend it and show it some gratitude. But best of all, I know the darkness will pass.

> *"Everything has its wonders, even the darkness and silence. And I learn, whatever state I may be in, therein to be content"*
> *Helen Keller*

What I hope to impart to the teens at the shelter, and all my fellow travelers to boot, is that life is indeed a magnificent smorgasbord of experiences. How lucky are we to have this chance to learn, to grow, to enjoy, to cry, to laugh, to mourn, to celebrate, to be anything we want, or to simply merely be. How splendid that if we can approach everything with LOVE (most importantly ourselves) we can't go wrong—period. It's true. No matter how awful things get, try throwing some love at it. Come on. Try it.

I haven't found everything that I'm looking for, but the painful, eye-opening life lessons that I've learned from the various "blood sucking monsters" in my life have set me on a path to living a full life, holding nothing but gratitude and big, bubbly, bountiful, beautiful love in my heart.

Now that I'm reconnected to myself and have genuine compassion for myself, all I want from this point forward in my life is to treat everyone and everything with loving-kindness. Yes, yes, it's major mushy stuff, but for me, it boosts my day. Every interaction I have is a chance to make the world a better place, and each loving connection makes me feel more and more wonderful. Holy macaroni. This is fantastic. This is <u>love</u>. I shit you not.

Hopefully from here, lovely reader, I can Oingo Boingo the whole way home, myself.

Useful Links for those in need of Help:
There are many different places that offer help—please don't think you have to go it alone.
The National Suicide Prevention Lifeline 1-800-273-8255.

Suicide is the third leading cause of death among 15 to 24-year-olds, and every day, roughly 5000 young people (in grades 7 to 12) attempt suicide in the USA. Sadly, these statistics have been steadily increasing over the years.

The USA is also in the midst of an opioid overdose epidemic. The sharp uptick in deaths coincides with Americans' increasing use of drugs like fentanyl, a pain reliever that is 100 times as strong as morphine and 30-50 times more powerful than heroin. No, no! Don't be tempted.

A person dies every 29 minutes, every day, from opioid poisoning. That's crazy right? Das ist verrückt. C'est fou dans la tête. Eso es súper loco. In every language—it's madness

The Substance Abuse and Mental Health Services Administration (SAMSHA) runs a free 24-hour hot line for treatment referrals and support: 1-800-662-HELP (4357). Calls are confidential and offered in English and Spanish. https://www.samhsa.gov

The Partnership for Drug Free Kids has a toll-free hot line (1-855-DRUGFREE) for parents who are seeking help for their children.
http://www.drugfree.org/get-help

The Children's Institute—http://www.childrensinstitute.org
The First Place for Youth—http://www.firstplaceforyouth.org
My friend's Place—http://myfriendsplace.org
Larkin Street Youth Services—http://larkinstreetyouth.org
The Trevor Project—https://www.thetrevorproject.org
Saving Teens—http://savingteens.org
The Teen line—https://teenlineonline.org

Shout-out to Rob Scheer who was in and out of foster homes himself as a child. All Rob had to hold his belongings as a kid was a trash bag, so later, as an adult, when he adopted several children himself, he was shocked when they too arrived with their belongings in trash bags.

"How could it be that over 30 years later we still had not gotten it right? How were we still asking children to pack up their life in a trash bag? Where is the dignity in that for a child who is scared and vulnerable?"

Rob started an organization called *Comfort Cases*, which since its inception has distributed over 18,000 cases to children in the Maryland, DC, and Virginia areas. The cases include pajamas, a blanket, a stuffed animal, a book, a dental kit, a hygiene kit, and a fun activity (coloring book and crayons, journal with pens/pencils).

Please support Rob Scheer and the other 428,000 foster children and at-risk youth out there. http://comfortcases.org

ACKNOWLEDGEMENTS

Please know that if I come across as flippant or callous, that is partly my writing style, and partly a coping method I use to navigate my world. Let me assure you that having worked with emotionally fragile teens for 18 years, I know firsthand how vulnerable they are, and I feel for them deeply. Their individual plights helped light the way for me during my own "dark" times, and for that I am extremely grateful. I learned so much by working with them and I hope they benefited from my presence, too.

It may also bother some of you that I never supply the conclusions to these teen's life stories, but honestly, I don't know how they end. The teens come and go very quickly. We only offer a 3-week stay and some teens only manage a few days, some merely a few hours. We do follow up with the client for a brief moment to see how they are doing, but most times, we can't get ahold of the family. They've moved, or the phone number is no longer valid. These are families in crisis, so not surprisingly, they are unstable.

Some of the teens mentioned in this book will be in their late twenties and early thirties by now. I sincerely hope that they have found their footing and are enjoying life to the max.

I'd like to send an enormous shout out to all the underpaid and overworked staff members in social services everywhere. It's an exhausting, never-ending job, and I bow to you all for your service.

Huge kudos to Colleen, the shelter's director. It is her loving energy and boundless good cheer that keep the shelter afloat.

And to Ben, for his tireless commitment to never-ever let anyone down. You are an exceptional human being, Ben—and thank you for covering my ass so many times at the shelter.

To Roy Hoffman I send nothing but love. I know this is a one-sided view of him (my side), and for all his generosity and the wondrously enjoyable moments, I cannot say thank you enough. Roy, I truly hope you are content wherever you are.

And last, but not least, to my brave, honest, decent-to-the core daughter, Samantha. I am massively proud of you, and love you beyond. Beyond, beyond.

Oh, and a last shout out to all you single parents. Keep up the good work. I'm on the other end of that journey now, and holy-baby-Moses-in-a-wicker-basket is it worth it. Seriously. Yes!

Thank you Roy for opening my heart.
Thank you shelter teens for opening my eyes.

www.ingramcontent.com/pod-product-compliance
Lightning Source LLC
Chambersburg PA
CBHW070143100426
42743CB00013B/2806